Getting into College

Getting into College

A Guide
for Students and Parents

REVISED EDITION

Frank C. Leana

HILL AND WANG   NEW YORK
The Noonday Press

Library of Congress Cataloging-in-Publication Data
Leana, Frank C.
    Getting into college : a guide for students and parents / Frank C.
Leana.—Rev. ed.
        p.   cm.
    Includes bibliographical references.
    1. Universities and colleges—United States—Entrance
requirements—Handbooks, manuals, etc.   2. College, choice of—
United States—Handbooks, manuals, etc.   3. Education—United
States—Parent participation—Handbooks, manuals, etc.   I. Title.
    LB2351.2.L4   1990   378.1'057'0973—dc20   90-35914CIP

for Lenesa

Acknowledgments

I am grateful to many for their support and assistance over the years.

Some have helped by their influence, such as my mother and father and my aunts Beenie and Mary, who gave me every opportunity for an excellent education; Zachary, my stepson, who taught me to see my work from a parental point of view; and Linus, my desk-side muse.

Others assisted me directly, lending help and encouragement as I wrote this new edition: Carole Clark and Connie Lufrano; Howard Greene, from whom there is always something new to learn about educational counseling; and Arthur Wang, editor and friend, who made this book possible.

Special thanks to the following students for allowing me to include their model writing: Elizabeth Beil, Jason Bordoff, Jessica Clark, J. Dennis Derryberry, Alexander Spelman, Anthony Sterns, Sara Thomas, and Wesley Thurman.

NEW YORK, NEW YORK
February 1990

Contents

PART TWO: Getting There

Introduction

The first edition of *Getting into College* arrived in the bookstores in 1980. The early 1980s were a time of relative innocence in the field of college admissions. Students and others involved in the process seemed to have a better gauge of what colleges were "looking for" in an applicant. Most students began to think about the application process some time in the spring of their junior year, took the SAT in May and Achievement Tests in June, saw some colleges over the summer and early fall of senior year, and applied to five or six schools before the first of January. But in the second half of the 1980s a serpent entered the garden. Its name was "demographics." Demographics are the statistical data that explain the "average" behavior of a particular population. Demographics warned of a significant decline in the number of eighteen-year-olds which would, in turn, create a serious drop in college enrollments. Such announcements heralded a new era in college admissions.

Despite a 2% decline in the traditional college-age population as early as 1981, selective colleges that year saw record-level enrollments. These high numbers of applicants continued throughout the 1980s. While demographers anticipate a steady decline throughout the 1990s, selective colleges observe that those students who apply now are, by and large, more highly qualified than applicants of the past. Students desiring admission to these schools will continue to face stiff competition in the process. Several admissions directors from selective colleges commented at the end of the 1989 admissions year that students on their Wait List could have made up a freshman class as impressive as that made up of admitted students.

The contradiction that exists between declining numbers of eighteen-year-olds and record-breaking enrollments for the past five years in competitive college admissions might be explained by several factors. Our conservative social climate values a traditional college education. Parents want the most for their money—the best, most prestigious college their child can enter—and, along with their child, take a more active role in the selection of colleges they consider to give good value for the very considerable investment. Most important, colleges, hearing the trumpetings of demographers, shook hands with Madison Avenue to target specific potential audiences. These groups came from geographic regions previously untapped, such as the Northwest or Southeast, and from groups previously underrepresented: blue-collar families, minorities, women, and older students returning to complete their education. Colleges have shifted from elitism to choosing students with a diversity of background, interests, and commitments. Thousands of dollars are budgeted by colleges to create appealing catalogues that show cool blue summertime lakes in northern climates and ski slopes only miles from the desert, videos, and alumni network outreach programs. The admissions process has been stepped up and glamorized.

The Revised Edition of *Getting into College* appears ten years and six printings after the first edition. My objective continues to be to provide students and their families with a readable, clear, practical guide through the college application process. Much of what was true for the 1980s remains true for the 1990s. Most selective colleges prefer or require a certain core of traditional courses; deadlines exist for Early Action, Early Decision, or regular admissions; demonstrated leadership or talent remains an important part of any student profile; and SAT scores are still more significant at some colleges than at others. But many of the changes in the 1980s have brought increased uncertainty, confusion, and anxiety to counselors, families, and students alike. The Revised Edition emphasizes in the first section, "Getting Ready," the importance of long-range planning from middle school through twelfth grade—and perhaps beyond, in a postgraduate or alternative year before college.

This new edition considers the needs of specialized groups, such as foreign and learning disabled students. It offers insight and advice to families on understanding the emotional dynamics of applying to college and leaving home. Current application essay topics are listed, and examples of several complete essays are included here also.

Most important, perhaps, in a period of competitive admissions, the Revised Edition focuses on the applicant's need to distinguish his or her candidacy from the 11,708 others seen by a selective university. An updated selected bibliography lists those publications in my own counseling library that have proved reliable and useful.

Getting into College shows candidates how to make the most of high school opportunities, academic and social, and ultimately how to put themselves in the best possible position to get into the college of their choice. This approach begins by understanding the steps of the application process and one's own qualifications. It starts in ninth grade and takes you to the moment when you decide which college to attend.

The application process also demands a series of emotional responses at each step. To think about yourself—who you are and what you want to do in the next four years and thereafter—calls for self-evaluation. That can be confusing and painful as well as ultimately enlightening.

Getting into College discusses some of the reactions and responses that students and their families will experience throughout the senior year of high school as they proceed through the various stages of completing the application requirements. Applying to college is more than a technical process. It is a rite of passage that occurs at a particular stage of our development as we prepare to leave the familiarity of high school and family and set out into new physical, intellectual, social, and psychological landscapes.

My goal is to empower the applicant to control what can be controlled about the process and to realize and accept what cannot. My experience as a teacher of high school and college students for seventeen years, as a private high school college counselor for ten years, as an educational consultant with Howard Greene & Associates for five years, and as a stepparent for three years has kept me close to the concerns, questions, and feelings of students and parents. I interview and counsel them every workday. I know that, to take part in competitive college admission in the 1990s, candidates and their families must be even more careful about the college they select and how they convey a truthful, individualized presentation of themselves. Families need to be informed and reassured. I hope that *Getting into College* will be of help.

PART ONE

Getting Ready

Concerns about College

I AM standing in the lunch line at a private day school on a professional visit. Next to me, heaping hot dogs onto their trays, two seventh-grade boys in dapper navy blazers and repp ties engage in obvious camaraderie. One boy turns to the other and asks, "Alex, where do you want to go to college?" "Princeton," replies Alex, his expression dimming as the conversation turns serious. "Oh," responds Ted, "me, too! I guess that means we can be friends for about another two years before we become competitors."

Returning from her doctor's office, where she has heard the good news, an excited mother-to-be reaches for the telephone to dial the office of the dean of admissions at an Ivy League university. "Where should we enroll our son or daughter in preschool so that admission to your college will be guaranteed?" she asks.

A young urban couple sits at the table with their six-year-old daughter. Tomorrow Mindy will face her interviewer at a highly selective, prestigious private school known for its outstanding college placement record over the years. In front of Mindy is a bowl of what looks like pasta. The couple has heard that one typical question for admission into first grade is "What is your favorite vegetable?" Fearful that Mindy will answer with a response as mundane as corn or potatoes, her parents are introducing her to the more exotic "spaghetti squash."

3

* * *

Concern about getting children into college begins in some families at the time their children are born, or even before, as in one of the cases above. Such hopes for opportunity in the years ahead are inherent in the American Dream, and a college diploma is thought to lead to personal and professional success. College is the final step of late adolescence of an elaborate plan, sometimes unspoken but dreamed, that begins years earlier. Is it any wonder that the application process becomes so highly charged with emotions ranging from excitement to anxiety and disappointment?

I suggest that instead of thinking about *where* you go to college as the most important decision of your life, you think of it as one very important decision. It may well be, for some of you, the biggest decision you have yet had to make about your future. But, remember, family, teachers, counselors, and professionals exist who can help you to make the best decisions about college. You do not have to make the journey alone.

With this view in mind, you as a family will want to begin planning after eighth grade. Being aware of what goes into a college application and of what colleges look for in deciding to admit or deny a candidate is one way to think about how you can get the most out of your high school years. No student should plan the high school experience merely to "look good" to colleges. However, thoughtful consideration about how to develop your academic and extracurricular interests and to strengthen your personal values through commitment to activities and to others does enrich the high school years and, at the same time, prepares you to succeed in the college application process.

The Advantage of Early Planning

W HEN should a family begin thinking about college for their son or daughter? The student who begins to think about college in the fall of senior year is too late to do much to alter the range of colleges that will admit him. Getting ready for college actually begins before the eleventh or twelfth years of school. It begins with a student's choice of courses and academic performance in the ninth grade. Partly because of high costs and partly because of the ever-increasing significance of a college education, parents are asking earlier how they can help their child to plan ahead to get the most out of the high school experience. Students who are successful and do well in high school will emerge from the educational process not only well adjusted but more likely to succeed in the college placement process because they know who they are and can begin to communicate their security to others. How the child learns and grows and changes is increasingly becoming as important to colleges as where or what he or she has studied. A family needs to ask what the likelihood is that given a certain school environment their child will be encouraged to develop a commitment to, and ideally a love of, learning, a social conscience, a solid set of moral and ethical values, and an awareness of the larger world around them. Which is the right curriculum to choose, balanced with the appropriate choices of Honors and Advanced Placement courses, electives, and traditional required offerings such as foreign language and calculus that will not only educate in a broad and deep way but will encourage growth in new fields as well? What we the parents as well as colleges will want to know down the road is, have the students been able to take advantage of the opportunities available to them and have they grown to reach beyond themselves to address the lives of others through leadership and public service?

SELECTING COURSES WITH COLLEGE IN MIND

The first step in the college application process is to develop your individual strengths in your high school academic subjects, extra-curricular interests, and personal values. Colleges will ask what you personally have made of your opportunities and resources. Everyone's circumstances are different, but one fact is universally true: students who explore and come to know their strengths are more likely to develop them in college than students who do not engage in such self-evaluation.

There is a big difference between anxiety and pressure of the kind expressed in the three anecdotes that introduce the section "Concerns about College" and the healthy concern that comes from looking ahead and getting ready to apply to college in the senior year. Anxiety and thoughtless ambition can turn members of a family into basket cases. The strength that comes from healthy, constructive long-range planning will put you in the best possible position to enter the college of your choice.

Getting into college begins with the courses you select for ninth grade. When a college admissions committee reviews your application, it will look at your high school transcript, which lists the courses you have taken and the final grade you have received in each. Some high schools record trimester or semester grades.

Colleges place considerable importance on your junior year because it is the last full academic year before you apply that they can evaluate. They look to see that you have maintained or strengthened your performance from ninth grade on. The first half of senior year is also taken into consideration. In combination, the junior year and the first part of senior year quite accurately predict

AUNT JUDE'S
SKETCH PAD
Save 40%!

your capacity for independent work and success in your freshman year of college.

The most effective applications are those that demonstrate continuity of course selection, some variety among those selections, and follow-through. Continuity means selecting courses that follow a sequence: for instance, algebra, geometry, pre-calculus, and calculus; or biology, chemistry, physics, and advanced physics. You need to exhibit your willingness to pursue the study of a subject to the highest level offered at your high school at which you can do well. Sequential courses are especially important for specific career preparation in college; for example, a premed student will need a strong background in math and science. At most colleges you will be required to declare a major concentration after sophomore year. Sequences in high school afford you the opportunity to delve deeply into a subject in much the same way as you will do in college.

Variety means experimenting with some courses outside of the traditional core of offerings, such as music appreciation, art history, theater, or astronomy. It is a mistake to specialize too quickly. Exploring courses outside your primary academic interest demonstrates your openness to new intellectual experiences. In college you will have many opportunities to reach out to a new subject such as anthropology or Swahili. If you would like to try a course in economics but are worried that your result might hurt your overall grade point average, consider a Pass/Fail option offered for electives at some high schools or perhaps an Audit, where you sit in on classes and do all of the assignments but do not receive a grade. Such options should be in addition to, not a substitute for, a graded normal course load. Any course such as Ceramics, Driver's Education, or Health should also complement but not be in lieu of traditional academic offerings.

Follow-through means taking your interest beyond the textbook and the classroom to involvement in a related extracurricular activity. If you are enrolled in a theater course, consider taking on even a small part in the school production. If you enjoy writing, join the staff of the school newspaper or the literary magazine. Put your skill in photography to use as yearbook photographer, or your interest in economics to the test by joining the business staff of a school organization. Colleges respond positively when you demonstrate your capacity to apply what you have learned to school and community life.

The outline on pp. 10–11 is a flexible curriculum plan for grades nine through twelve. Notice that math, science, and a foreign language are ideally taken through a three- or four-year sequence, as competitive colleges report an increase in their applicants' study of foreign languages, laboratory sciences, and computer science courses.

Computer science should not be viewed as a substitute for courses in pure mathematics, but it would be better to have taken an elective in computer science than no course in the quantitative subjects. Many colleges, such as Carnegie-Mellon or Dartmouth, require of all freshmen a working knowledge of computers.

The course plan outline will help you avoid any regret you might feel as a junior for what you haven't tried or accomplished. There is no point in regretting your omissions or mistakes; take positive action in the time that is left and make senior year count heavily.

High school should not be viewed merely as a stepping-stone to college, but rather as a rich developmental stage of your life. It is a time for intellectual growth, social maturation, and personal realization. Although colleges look for leaders and scholars, they want students who have learned to enjoy what they do, whose involvements have enriched their lives and their value systems.

Show in your application that you think about what you do. Underscore strengths and accomplishments by using detail. Put your achievements and values forward in the best yet honest light. For instance, it is not sufficient to mention that you are editor or sports writer on the school newspaper. Give a sense of how frequently the paper comes out and of how important the club or organization is at your school. You should not assume that colleges will necessarily know that being elected to an office in a particular organization at your school is a big deal. You need to tell them if it is.

Colleges are wary of students who cannot set priorities in high school, who spread themselves too thin. In the independent atmosphere of college, you will need to organize your time effectively and show good judgment in the choices you make.

Do not overload your schedule to look impressive. Choose courses carefully and do your best in them. It makes no sense to choose a course at an Advanced or Advanced Placement* level if you cannot do well. You need to be competent in the course and be able to meet its demands. And keep in mind that courses with labs, studio, and practice hours will call for even more hours of your time.

Students frequently wonder if it is more advisable to take fewer courses and get more A's and B's or to take more courses and perhaps get lower grades. Of course, there are many students who can take a heavy load of rigorous courses *and* get A's. However, you must assess realistically your own capacity to do your best work with a particular selection of courses. Each college applicant is evaluated according to what he or she has made of his or her particular opportunity. In a time when so much has been made of SAT scores and grade point averages, it should be viewed as a sign of hope that individual differences still matter.

* Advanced Placement, or AP, exams are given by the College Entrance Examination Board each May in the following subjects: American History, Art (includes a student portfolio), Art History, Biology, Chemistry, Computer Science, English Language, English Literature, European History, French Language, French Literature, German Language, Latin-Virgil, Latin-Catullus and Horace, Mathematics–Calculus AB (two levels), Mathematics–Calculus BC (two levels), Music Listening and Literature, Music Theory, Physics-B (two levels), Physics-C (two levels), Spanish Language, and Spanish Literature. Exams are scored on a scale of 1 to 5 (top). Some colleges accept a 3 for credit; most expect a 4 or 5, especially if you are seeking higher-level courses.

Sample Four-Year Curriculum Plan

	9	10	11	12
ENGLISH	English	English	English	Honors English
			Honors or AP English	English Electives
MATH	Algebra I	Algebra II	Geometry	Pre-Calculus
				Business Math
	Algebra II	Geometry	Pre-Calculus	Calculus AB or BC
				Probability and Statistics
SCIENCE	Biology	Chemistry	Physics	AP ⎰ Biology, Chemistry, or Physics ⎱
	Intro. to Physical Science	Biology	Chemistry	Physics

	Latin II	Latin III	Latin AP	Latin AP
LANGUAGE	French Italian Spanish German Japanese or Chinese Russian	Three years of one foreign language are preferred to two years each of two languages		
HISTORY	Ninth-grade History / Ancient Civilization	Modern European History / Modern European History AP	American History / American History AP	Electives: Contemporary, Latin American, African
ARTS	Two credits over four years from among electives such as Studio Art, Music, Dance, Theater, Ceramics, Jewelry-Making, Photography, and Art History			
PHYSICAL EDUCATION	PE	PE	PE	PE

Developing Extracurricular Interests

SOME seniors take a look at the section of an application where they are asked to list their activities and turn pale. They worry that they do not have an impressive list. However, colleges believe that it is more important to make a commitment to a few activities and do them well than to spread yourself too thin. Persistence in an activity has been shown to lead to both academic and social success in college. Many of the essay and interview questions you will be asked to answer will probe to see if your involvements and commitments have helped you to develop a system of personal values. For instance, an essay topic used by many colleges asks you to discuss your most significant extracurricular activity or interest and its influence on you.

Colleges are not impressed by a laundry list of activities. Rather, they want to learn how you have made a difference to a team or organization and how being a part of an activity has led to your development and your self-understanding.

> *The strength of your high school curriculum and the grades you earn are the two most significant factors in your application to any college. The ways in which you have used your time are important criteria, after course selection and grade point average.*

Summer Activities and Alternatives

TRAVEL AND STUDY

COLLEGES are interested in how you have used your time. Once you have selected an academic program that is appropriately demanding and made choices about what activities and outside-of-school interests you want to pursue, you will need to think about a resourceful use of summer vacations.

Junkets across Europe or Australia with your parents or a pack of teens do not in themselves impress college admissions deans. First of all, anyone with the money can sign up and participate. There is little evidence of resourcefulness in simply enjoying the sights. While there is no one activity in itself that registers a high rating, activities that call for independence, exploration of talents and interests, the formal study of subjects or a culture and language, assistance to others as a teacher or counselor on a volunteer basis, or sticking to an old-fashioned job for the first time do command attention.

The travel programs that increase your admission chances combine some element of cultural exposure or academic study with travel. The summer after junior year might be an ideal time to pursue one of these programs.

What follow are some well-known commercial organizations that sponsor summer travel and study programs. The list is by no means exhaustive but gives an idea of the variety available.

American Institute for Foreign Studies
102 Greenwich Avenue
Greenwich, Connecticut 06830

These summer study programs are carefully planned at well-known European and Asian universities. They range from three to twelve weeks in length. There are separate high school divisions. Cost runs between approximately $2,000 and $4,000, depending on the cost of transportation and the length of the program.

The Experiment in International Living
Putney, Vermont 05346

This program offers summer and semester homestays for high school students, some of which include attendance at a local school abroad. Students live with native prescreened families to pursue particular aspects of a culture.

Academic Study Abroad
400 Main Street
Armonk, New York 10504

This organization offers educational travel programs that immerse American high school students in a learning environment, such as St. Clare's in Oxford; a London arts program where students work side by side with professionals in theater studio art, creative writing, architecture, and film and television studies; language study and a three-week homestay with a French family; a British culture and society program; and language programs in Spain, Germany, and Italy.

A part of Academic Study Abroad is the popular five-week pre-college enrichment at Amherst College. High school students are housed at Amherst in dormitories and select one major academic course and one elective. Among the electives is an SAT preparation course run by Princeton Review.

Greek Summer
380 Madison Avenue
New York, New York 10017

The focus of this work-travel program sponsored by the American Farm School near Thessaloníki, Greece, is a work project in a local village. Projects are practical and improve the life of the villagers, such as paving streets or working farms. Greek Summer is open to students entering grades eleven or twelve or who have just been graduated. The six-week program has a break at the end of the first three weeks that involves travel to Athens, classical Greece, and a Greek island.

Ithaka
Box 1420
Back Bay Annex
Boston, Massachusetts 02117

Ithaka offers semester and five-week summer programs in Greece that include academic study of Greek culture, intensive reading and writing, an archaeological field trip, an introduction to modern Greek, and apprenticeships with local craftsmen on the island of Kálimnos. The semester option is for students from the ages of sixteen to nineteen; the summer program for students from thirteen to fifteen.

Putney Travel
Putney, Vermont 05346

Putney Travel supervises small groups of students completing tenth, eleventh, or twelfth grade on five-to-six-week-long tours in Europe, Australia and New Zealand, Canada, and the Soviet Union. Putney emphasizes the importance of active participation in the life and culture of the country. Experiences range from a bike trip through Denmark to farm work in Normandy.

Tennis: Europe
146 Cold Spring Road
Unit 13
Stamford, Connecticut 06905

This association offers tours for young men and women from the ages of fourteen to eighteen of varsity-, state-, or sectionally ranked ability in tennis. Students travel in three to six European countries and participate in four tournaments for up to a month. Trips leave at various times throughout the summer.

COLLEGE CAMPUS EXPERIENCES

Summer courses offered by colleges and universities are an excellent opportunity for you to experience dormitory living, the independence of college life, and study at the college level. You will also experience the diversity represented by most summer school populations. If you think you are interested in a particular college or in a particular kind of school (urban, rural, large, small), summer programs offer a tryout period to introduce you to each other.

Students often ask if going to a college's summer program gives them a foot in the door to regular admission. Unfortunately, the answer is usually no. The reasons to attend summer school, at either a boarding school or a college, are primarily

- to expand your knowledge of a particular subject.
- to explore new disciplines, such as psychology, archaeology, theater, and economics, which are not always offered in high school. For instance, Yale Summer School has offered Swahili.
- to strengthen and develop writing skills.
- to take a study skills course or SAT prep program, such as that at Tufts University or Ithaca College.

- to take a third or fourth lab science such as physics, particularly when scheduling it in your senior year would threaten your overall grade point average or when there is no available time in your school-year schedule.
- to practice and develop a talent such as sculpture, poetry writing, musical or dance performance, or computer science. Many summer programs in the arts exist, such as the Berkshire Center for the Performing Arts, the National Music Camp at Interlochen, Michigan, and the Marlboro Music Festival. There are also camps that specialize in every interest, from figure skating to canoeing. Consult your local newspaper for ads; *The New York Times Magazine* contains one of the most complete camp and summer opportunities listings.
- to make up a disappointing or failing grade in a subject or to fill a gap, such as an arts course or a course in math or science or language.

Applying to a summer school program serves as a trial run for the college application process. And asking teachers, principals, and counselors for recommendations is a precursor of those tasks ahead. Attending summer school allows you to demonstrate your seriousness about an academic interest or talent and your ability to handle college-level work.

A highly popular and successful residential and day program for teens is Exploration held on the campus of Wellesley College in Wellesley, Massachusetts. There is an intermediate program for students entering grades seven through nine and a senior program for students entering grades ten through twelve. Students attend two workshops of their choice a day on topics as diverse as public speaking and literature to engineering and oceanography. The program includes extracurricular activities, an SAT preparation course in the senior program, and evening and weekend activities ranging from trips to Boston or Tanglewood to visits to local colleges for those in the senior program.

Keystone Junior College sponsors Nokomis, a five-week summer (including the summer after graduation) group living experience in La Plume, Pennsylvania, for any high school junior or senior. The program combines academic study, sports, and physical work on environmentally related projects. Students are paid for one hundred work hours, and a part of these earnings go toward tuition. Students live in Keystone dormitories.

For students sixteen or over who are considering a career in the design professions—architecture, urban planning, landscape architecture—Harvard University offers Career Discovery. Held at the Graduate School of Design, Career Discovery courses integrate tutored studio practice, lectures, career advising, athletic and cultural activities, and field trips. Some colleges will accept this course of study for academic credit.

The Grinnell College Summer Institute in Grinnell, Iowa, introduces students to a new language, creative and research writing, and mathematical problem-solving and pre-calculus.

The Center for Creative Youth is a five-week residential offering held at Wesleyan University in Middletown, Connecticut. It is open to high school students entering grades ten through twelve. Students participate in daily three-hour sessions in an area of major interest and in two-hour interdisciplinary sessions combining art forms, such as creative writing, dance, theater, or music. At the end of a residency, students are encouraged to design and execute a year-long project to enrich the arts at their schools.

Summer in New York is Barnard College's pre-college, four-week session for highly motivated students who have completed eleventh grade. Each student selects two academic courses taught by Barnard faculty. In supervised evening and weekend programs, students explore recreational and cultural attractions of the city.

The Bennington July Program, held on the Bennington College campus in Bennington, Vermont, exists to help students who have completed sophomore or junior year of high school to work in music, dance, drama, acting, painting, ceramics, photography, languages, mathematics, and pre-medical and pre-law studies. Learning takes place in tutorials and small classes and is in-depth.

The Bennington Writing Workshops, also held on the Bennington campus, is one of the most highly regarded writing workshops in the country. The program consists of workshops, readings, and informal meetings with writers. Workshops are offered in two- or four-week sessions, and enrollment is limited.

The Johns Hopkins University Center for the Advancement of Academically Talented Youth offers summer programs for verbally and mathematically talented young people from the ages of twelve to sixteen and a half. Sessions are held on campuses in California, Pennsylvania, Maryland, and New York. The Center conducts regional, national, and international talent searches to identify students in as early as the seventh grade who score at least as high on the SAT as an average college-bound high school senior. Courses spanning the humanities, mathematics, and computer science are conducted at a challenging level. A high degree of motivation and self-discipline is expected of students.

The Washington Workshops (1-800-368-5688) offer programs for high school students that focus on politics. Three one-week sessions are held in New York City on Wall Street and emphasize the American business and financial system.

Boarding schools also offer exciting summer programs, but thes might be more appropriate for a younger student since these se sions are more supervised than most of those held on coll campuses. In addition to traditional offerings, many schools summer instruction to foreign students in English as a Se Language, such as Cushing Academy in Ashburnham, M chusetts, or the Delphian School in Sheridan, Oregon; stud and writing development, such as the outstanding summ gram at the Salisbury School in Salisbury, Connecticut Webb School in Claremont, California; or remedial work or English.

When you think about summer-study possibilities, se gram and locale you are interested in and will enjoy. Tl should be a time of renewal, not a grind. It is a mist some exotic study you think will impress college adn

will get more out of an experience you look forward to and will talk and write about it more effectively if you have valued it than if you have merely done what you think, or your parents think, you should do to please colleges.

It is important to keep in mind that scholarships are available for most summer programs if you demonstrate financial need. Do not assume that a college summer program would be cost prohibitive.

OUTDOORS ADVENTURES

Another category of summer experience includes programs that feature encounters with the great outdoors. Such programs are designed to encourage and develop self-confidence, leadership, and a spirit of cooperation in natural settings. Programs range in length from a few days to a month or longer.

Outward Bound
384 Field Point Road
Greenwich, Connecticut 06830

At Outward Bound, the oldest adventure-based program in the United States, the outdoors becomes a natural classroom in which instructors and fellow participants engage in a sequence of events to stretch you physically, mentally, and emotionally. Exercises are designed to encourage you to take charge, discover leadership within yourself, and develop a sense of teamwork and community. Outward Bound schools are located in North Carolina, Maine, Minnesota, Colorado, and Oregon. Some courses are open to students as young as fourteen.

Earthwatch Expeditions, Inc.
680 Mount Auburn Street
Box 403
Watertown, Massachusetts 02272

Earthwatch offers adventure/research expeditions as diverse as archaeology in Majorca and health care in a Nepal village, for students sixteen and over. Besides Watertown, Earthwatch has offices in Sydney, Australia; Pacific Palisades, California; San Antonio, Texas; and Washington, D.C.

National Outdoor Leadership School
P.O. Box AA
Lander, Wyoming 82520

NOLS offers over forty courses in five countries (Mexico, Argentina, the U.S.–Alaska, Kenya, and Tanzania) on three continents. The curriculum introduces young people to wilderness skills, conservation, and leadership. Courses range in length from two weeks to an entire semester. The NOLS philosophy stresses the importance of sound decision-making in wilderness environments as different as the Wind River Range of Wyoming and the coastline of the Sea of Cortés. Minimum age for some programs is fifteen.

Keewaydin Canoe Trips
4242 Brookdale Street
Jackson, Mississippi 39206

Based in Ontario, Canada, this program offers sessions of six or seven weeks to young men or three weeks to boys ages ten and eleven, in which a group of campers pitch tent, fish, canoe, compete in sports, and explore the Canadian wilderness.

Yosemite Institute
Box 487
Yosemite National Park, California 95389

The institute offers summer courses for high school students that range from hikes and backpacking trips to classes emphasizing natural history, geology, and astronomy.

SUMMER EMPLOYMENT

Students often ask if it is okay to stay at home and get a job during the summer after tenth or eleventh grade. Work experience is very valuable, both in itself and as an experience in the "real world" of getting along with bosses and fellow workers. As I have said earlier, much more important than specifically what you do is that colleges want to know how you have spent your summers and what the experience has meant to you. So, if working in a store, learning about the inner workings of a law office, or adjusting to the pace and rigorous schedule of a fast-food clerk gives you a meaningful experience to talk and write about, then that is just as acceptable as going off to a college campus or the wilderness. Any of the experiences discussed above are only as valuable as your appreciation of them.

The suggestions I have made in this section are by no means comprehensive. They are merely some of the more popular choices with proven track records of providing successful summer experiences for young people. Entire books are devoted to listings of summer travel and learning experiences, camps, outdoor programs, and travel and study abroad. Some are listed in the Selected Bibliography. The rest you can locate in a research section of a public or school guidance library or in bookstores.

Standardized Testing

A LMOST every student who applies to college will face standardized entrance examinations, beginning with the Preliminary Scholastic Aptitude Test (PSAT), continuing with the Scholastic Aptitude Test (SAT) or the American College Test (ACT), and concluding with one or more Achievement Tests.

THE PSAT

Many high schools recommend that their students take the PSAT in the fall of their sophomore year for practice. But most students will take it officially in the fall of their junior year, usually in October. The exam is announced in advance, and juniors take it as a class. There is no preregistration.

The PSAT is a two-hour exam that tests your ability to reason with verbal and mathematical symbols. You will receive in advance a practice test and bulletin of information. When scores are returned to the high school, each student receives an answer key and a copy of his or her original answer sheet. Schools will return the question booklets, so in effect you can go over your errors and learn from them. Many commercial review books exist that will familiarize you with the format of the PSAT and perhaps increase your confidence as a standardized-test-taker. The PSAT results are returned with an elaborate computer printout that helps you to assess what your scores mean and what projections you can make for the SAT results based on the PSAT scores. A separate score is given for the verbal and the mathematics sections of the exam.

By meeting certain eligibility requirements stated in section 10 of the PSAT answer sheet, a student taking the PSAT may compete for scholarships under the National Merit Scholarship Program and the National Achievement Scholarship Program for Outstanding Negro Students.

If your scores qualify you, you may be declared a scholarship semifinalist in September of your senior year. You must rank in the top one-half of one percent of your state to be a semifinalist. A high PSAT score also identifies you to colleges. You may receive a letter from the National Merit Scholarship Corporation in the spring of your junior year inviting you to have your scores sent to two colleges of your choice. This alerts these two colleges early to your interest in them.

When you register for the PSAT, decide what form of your name you wish to use on future standardized test registrations. If you use Samuel Z. White on one registration and S. Zachary White on another, you may well have trouble later collecting all your scores on one printout.

THE SAT

Over one million students take the Scholastic Aptitude Test (SAT) each year. It is requested by over 70% of the nation's colleges. The SAT is a three-hour-long, multiple-choice test made up of two verbal and two mathematical sections (thirty minutes long each), a Test of Standard Written English (TSWE) (thirty minutes), and one experimental section (thirty minutes). The experimental section is unspecified and does not affect your score but is used for test measurement purposes. It may appear on your exam in the format of mathematical, verbal, or TSWE questions. Each section is separately timed and scored on a scale of 200 (low) to 800 (high). Verbal sections test reasoning ability using antonyms, sentence completions, analogies, and reading comprehension passages. Math sections test your knowledge of arithmetic, algebra, and geometry. The TSWE tests the ability to recognize errors in English grammar and usage.

You should plan to take the SAT in either March or May of your junior year. Taking it in March means that you will receive your scores before the end of school and can do some important planning with your counselor about how best to use the summer to visit colleges. However, depending upon your curriculum and your own readiness to do your best on the SAT, you may find that the extra couple of months gives you more time to feel confident. For one thing, you will have covered more math in class by May. If you have taken the SAT by the end of your junior year, you will have left the fall and winter test dates open during your senior year in case you wish to retake either the SAT or an Achievement Test in time to have it considered with your applications.

Students ask if they should guess on the SAT when they do not know the answer for certain. Since the SAT is scored on the basis of the number of questions you answer correctly minus a fraction of the number you answer incorrectly, uneducated guessing is unlikely to change your score for the better. If you can intelligently eliminate one or more of the choices from among five, however, educated guessing could improve your score.

If you have completed your standardized testing, at least one time through, by the end of your junior year, you are in an ideal position to consider applying for Early Decision or Early Action (see pp. 81–82) should that become of interest to you after you have visited some colleges. With test scores in hand, you can begin to visit colleges with some sense of where you stand in relation to the rest of the competition. This information will enable your interviewers to help you assess your chances of being admitted to particular schools.

THE ACT

The American College Test is made up of four sections: English (forty-five minutes), mathematics (sixty minutes), reading (thirty-five minutes), and science reasoning (thirty-five minutes). This exam measures the knowledge and skills you have developed from grades seven through eleven. The scores are a composite of these four fields and are reported from a low of 1 to a high of 36. For many years the ACT was used by colleges and universities located in the Midwest, West, and South. In the past few years, colleges in the East and middle-Atlantic states have increasingly suggested that students may want to take both the SAT and the ACT to see on which of the two they perform better.

Some colleges will accept either, and you can choose which score to have sent. If standardized testing proves troublesome to you, you at least ought to get acquainted with the format and content of the ACT and SAT by reading their information bulletins and checking out a commercial review book to see if you perform better, or with less anxiety, on one test than the other.

To obtain information bulletins on the ACT and SAT, write

ACT Registration Department
P.O. Box 414
Iowa City, Iowa 52243
"Preparing for the ACT Assessment"
and "Contents of the Tests in the ACT Assessment"

The College Board ATP
P.O. Box 6200
Princeton, New Jersey 08541-6200
"SAT and Achievement Tests"

Many commercial books exist to acquaint you with sample questions and test-taking strategies. I will not give examples from them here. My purpose in *Getting into College* is rather to discuss when these exams ought to be taken, how colleges use them in evaluating your candidacy, and how you should prepare to take standardized tests.

ACHIEVEMENT TESTS

The Achievement Test is one hour in length and may be taken in fifteen different subject areas: English Composition, with or without Essay, English Literature, Mathematics Level I or Level II, American History and Social Studies, European History and World Cultures, Biology, Chemistry, Physics, French, German, Modern Hebrew, Italian, Latin, and Spanish. Math Level I is a survey of three years of college preparatory mathematics; Math Level II is for students who have taken three and one-half years or more of college preparatory mathematics. As many as three Achievement Tests can be taken in one three-hour administration.

I recommend that every applicant to selective colleges plan to take three Achievements. The English Composition Achievement is required by most selective colleges. The other two choices should reflect your range of interests and abilities—for instance, one in math and one in language or history, or a science and a math if you are planning to concentrate in or choose a career in these fields.

In general, students find the American History and Social Studies and the English Literature Achievement Tests quite difficult. The history examination tests factual knowledge of political, social, economic, and diplomatic history. The English Literature test measures the ability to interpret prose, poetry, and dramatic literature and to identify elements of style as well as show familiarity with literary and critical terms such as *irony* and *satire*.

Barron's, an educational publishing company, has issued a review book for each Achievement Test subject. These review books are obtainable from bookstores or directly from Barron's Educational Series, Inc., 113 Crossways Park Drive, Woodbury, New York, 11797.

On the December test date, the English Composition Achievement Test includes a twenty-minute essay. If you write well on the spot, and prefer a chance to write an essay, you should register for the December test. Some colleges require or recommend that you take the Achievement with Essay. Be sure to check the particular requirements of those colleges to which you will be applying. Unless you are contemplating an Early Decision application, it is all right to take the English Composition Achievement with Essay in December of your senior year. You may want to take the regular English Composition in June of your junior year along with two others, and then add the December version if your choices require it. Essays are evaluated on the student's ability to present ideas clearly and logically in correct English. English teachers from high schools across the country meet as a group to evaluate these essays for the College Board, using scores of 0 to 4. No separate score is reported for the Essay, only the total score of 200 to 800. The score report does indicate that the student took the English Composition with Essay.

Some colleges that require or strongly recommend the English Composition with Essay will waive that recommendation for a candidate with a proven record of high achievement in English courses and demonstrated writing ability. It pays to check with your interviewer or with a call to an admissions counselor if you wonder whether or not you should plan to take the English Achievement with Essay. Students who write easily and well may prefer to take the December English Achievement because that test will have fewer multiple-choice grammar questions.

The College Board makes available free of charge through your high school guidance office the booklet "Taking the Achievement Tests," which contains brief samples of each subject test.

PREPARING FOR STANDARDIZED TESTS

Test scores are one important factor in the decision-making process at most selective colleges. SAT or ACT scores become a screening device at those colleges where the number of applicants far exceeds the number of students who can be offered admission. Other qualifications being equal among a group of applicants, SAT or ACT scores could be a deciding factor.

It has been demonstrated over time that those students who score at a certain level are more likely to perform successfully during freshman year. Indexes to colleges also list median SAT or ACT scores for each year's admitted freshmen. SAT or ACT scores are a part of a college's profile. Unfortunately, in my opinion, numbers such as these have too frequently become equated with quality and prestige. Institutions with high median scores are perforce thought to represent the best and the brightest. National rating surveys that group colleges competitively almost always factor test scores significantly in determining categories of selectivity. Test scores have become public relations and recruitment tools as well as measurements of aptitude and skills development.

Nevertheless, you will need to do your best on such standardized tests, as long as they remain a valued part of the application and admissions process at those colleges that interest you. Take them seriously and prepare for them.

No college should be eliminated from your list solely because of SAT or ACT score medians. Scores are only a part of your application. At some colleges, they are a more important part than at others. You need to know which colleges are flexible about scores and be sure to include colleges that have a range of score requirements. Score requirements are listed in college indexes and in college catalogues.

Most colleges view the verbal score as more indicative than the math score of your ability to do college-level work. Exceptions to this are of course colleges and programs with special emphasis on premed, math, science, business, engineering, or architecture. A discrepancy between high scores and average or low grades in your courses may well be viewed by colleges as your failure to use your inherent ability in the classroom.

Probably two of the toughest decisions you will make about standardized testing are 1) How many times should you take each test? and 2) Should you prepare by enrolling in one of the many coaching programs such as Stanley Kaplan or the Princeton Review, two of the largest of these kinds of organizations?

If you are disappointed by your first set of test scores, definitely consider taking them a second time. Selective colleges, especially, like to see that you have put forth your best effort toward these exams. Colleges will see all of your scores, because the official printout is cumulative; however, colleges will either average your verbal and your math scores separately or record the higher score from each set.

There are four basic ways to prepare short-term for the ACT or SAT exams:

1. Acquire official publications from the College Board or the American College Testing Program (see p. 26 for addresses). These pamphlets contain sample questions and basic test-taking advice, such as how to pace yourself and whether or not to guess.

The College Board also publishes a collection of actual SAT exams, titled 10 SATs. A scoring mechanism is included so that you can correct each exam and determine an approximate score.

These tests provide the most accurate way to familiarize yourself with the formats of SAT questions. Other commercially published workbooks use simulated questions, which may not always capture the subtlety and precision of actual SAT questions.

If you can discipline yourself to set aside time on a regular basis and work your way through several sample tests, this method will help acquaint you with standardized test directions and format for the least cost. You will also begin to add to your vocabulary words that appear with frequency on such tests.

2. Sign up for a professional course; these are available internationally. Some courses are particularly geared to teach you highly sophisticated strategies that cut time and help you to second-guess the test. Some students may also benefit from the group camaraderie, which generates its own competitiveness. Scheduled classes

become an incentive to keep up with workbook exercises. Diagnostic tests are administered periodically to help you check your progress. The Princeton Review program has a computer-scored system that analyzes each diagnostic exam to group the kinds of errors you are making and to make specific recommendations about where you still need to concentrate.

3. Work one-on-one with an individual tutor who will help you to straighten out specific difficulties that you determine between you. This is probably going to be the most costly method of preparation.

4. Use the computer software kits that exist to run yourself through vocabulary building and test practice.

It is safe to say that no one method of test preparation necessarily works for everyone, so look closely at what a course or tutor attempts to accomplish. What style do they use? Are you comfortable with their aims and methods of instruction?

The only remedy I know to battle test-taking anxiety is to practice and talk about your worry with tutors and professionals. There is no substitute for the long-term benefits of good reading habits and close attention to schoolwork. However, preparation of some kind for standardized testing can increase your familiarity with the test format. Knowing what to expect should increase your confidence.

A controversy does remain over the effectiveness of any standardized test to predict your success in college, and also over the effectiveness of coaching. Standardized tests, nonetheless, remain a real part of every high school student's life who plans to apply to college. Rather than stew about the need for such exams it is better to take a thoughtful course of action. There is no guarantee that test preparation will increase your scores, but if you are willing to invest the time and money, it can't hurt. If nothing else, you are bound to learn some new words, and with a little effort get psyched to attack the test with some methodology in hand. You will at least feel that you have done everything you can to do your best.

You may request that your SAT be returned to you with the test questions, for a fee of $10. The registration booklet will list those national administration dates for which the question-and-answer service exists. You may order this service at the time of registration or up to five months after the test date. This service provides one of the best means of seeing what kinds of errors you are making so you may learn from them.

After you take the SAT, you will wait about six weeks for your scores to be returned to you. You will see a separate verbal score and a separate math score. The verbal score will be broken down into separate categories of vocabulary and reading comprehension. There will be an individual score for the Test of Standard Written English. There will also be a national percentage score, telling you where you place in relation to other college-bound students across the country.

National averages reflect an enormously diverse student population. When comparing your scores with the national level, you should keep in mind your individual situation—whether you come from a public or private high school, where it is geographically— and note how these factors might affect your chances of admission at a particular college. Check the college's profile to see what percentage of their accepted students have scores like yours and whether that percentage differs by region or type of high school.

Placing in the ninety-fifth percentile can be deceiving. More important is where your scores stand in relation to the median or average SAT or ACT scores of freshmen enrolled in a particular college. If your score is above the median, your chances are, of course, better for gaining admission. An entry in a school profile or index may read as follows: "Test Scores: Middle 50% of enrolled freshmen have SAT verbal scores between 500 and 580 and SAT math scores between 450 and 570." To compare your scores to national averages, keep in mind that the 1989 average SAT nationwide was 427 verbal and 476 math. The 1989 average ACT score nationwide was 18.6.

TEST-TAKING SCHEDULE

Below is the test-taking schedule I recommend:

Tenth grade: Take the PSAT for practice.

Eleventh grade: In October, take the PSAT to qualify for National Merit Scholarship Qualifying Test.

These results will serve as a reliable guide to assess what work lies ahead of you before taking the SAT.

Spring of eleventh grade: Take either the March or May SAT, depending upon your readiness. Be sure you know what math you will be expected to have covered. If you need the extra course work to cover more math, the May date may be more advisable.

June, eleventh grade: Try to take as many Achievement Tests as you will need (up to three in one sitting) to have completed three (minimum) by the end of junior year.

The ACT may be taken in the spring of junior year or the fall and winter of senior year.

This schedule has several advantages. It leaves at least three test dates open in your senior year in case you decide to repeat any exams. It puts you in an ideal position to consider an early application in the fall of senior year should you find the college of your dreams over the summer. It allows you to apply to some colleges on a rolling admission basis (see p. 83), such as the University of Wisconsin or the University of Michigan, early in the fall and receive a response a few weeks later. If you are interested in one of these colleges, and you have your testing completed, you don't have to delay applying.

A few colleges, such as Union, Middlebury, and Bates, offer the option of submitting five Achievement Test results in lieu of SAT scores. If you need to do two in the fall, you will have that chance by planning ahead and beginning early.

Having taken your standardized tests at least once and knowing your results by midsummer also allows you to target schools to visit with more information about which colleges are appropriate. In your interviews, you can address knowledgeably your concerns about how your testing will affect your chances for admission.

APTITUDE TESTING

Some students find it helpful in assessing their educational and career goals to take aptitude tests. Aptitude testing measures one's natural talents for doing or learning to do certain kinds of tasks with facility. Such aptitudes might be for manual dexterity, memory for numbers, or musical or artistic ability. Since every job or position calls for certain aptitudes to be successful at that job, you are most likely to be satisfied by work that uses your particular aptitudes.

Aptitude testing is often a useful adjunct to help you choose a field of study or an appropriate type of school.

The Johnson O'Connor Research Foundation is one long-established organization with regional offices that administers aptitude testing.

Sorting through Possibilities

O NE of the things that makes the college application process so confusing is the number of alternatives you have. It is a mistake for most people to begin thinking about going to college with only one college in mind. There are well over two thousand colleges and universities in the United States alone. Some are four-year colleges of under two thousand students, such as Hamilton, Mount Holyoke, Reed, or Pomona. Others are large public universities with over forty thousand students, such as the University of Wisconsin or Indiana University. There are two-year or junior colleges, both public and private, such as Dean Junior College in Franklin, Massachusetts, or the State University of New York at Morrisville. Some colleges enroll only women, such as Smith, a few only men, such as Hampden-Sydney. There are also many interesting alternatives to college, such as the Dynamy Program or a postgraduate year at a boarding school or study abroad. In this section we shall explore some of these choices.

As you begin to think about life after high school you owe it to yourself to know about the choices ahead of you before committing to any one of them. The student transfer rate from college to college in the United States is over 50%. Although many of these changes are appropriate, such a high percentage suggests that too few students make the best choice in the first place.

You are bound to feel certain pressures from family, peers, friends, teachers, and society at large—each of whom thinks he or she knows what is best for you and each of them well intentioned. I hope you will factor many opinions into your thinking about the next step after high school, but I hope even more that the final decision will be your own. You are the one who will live and work and relax in the new environment for one to four years.

Why do students go to college? Today's college students respond that they decided to go on to college to get a better job, gain a general education, make new friends, experience diversity among people, and eventually make more money. Studies show that graduates with a college degree do make about 80% more in their first few years on the job than do graduates with only a high school diploma.

Thinking about a career need not, and ideally should not, rule out the values and opportunities that come with a liberal arts education. Liberal arts colleges do not specifically address "career." They encourage you to continue to explore the humanities, the sciences, and the arts, developing skill in analytical thinking, knowledge of classical and modern thinkers and ideas, facility in a foreign language and culture, and to experiment with disciplines new to most of you, such as anthropology, semiotics, or economics. A liberal education emphasizes critical and analytical thinking across these various fields before you decide to major or concentrate in any one of them. A liberal arts student will be expected to develop written and oral skills and master the techniques of research.

A high school senior or a beginning college student should not be overly concerned about not having a specific career goal in mind when selecting colleges. Over 60% of students change their career plans at least once, often twice, during their college years. While one objective of a liberal arts education is to develop and focus the abilities you already have, another is to provide opportunities for you to discover new interests and abilities. Look for colleges and academic programs that will force you to think rigorously and to challenge your own beliefs. College should give you skills to adapt to changes in the job market and help you develop interests that will sustain you throughout your life. Some studies show that liberal arts graduates lead more satisfied lives (and in many cases end up earning more money) because they have been encouraged to question values, develop personal interests, and become goal-oriented rather than be preoccupied with "success." They have learned how to synthesize and analyze information, to weigh cause and effect, to solve problems, and to put events into perspective.

Some students define their goals early in life because of a special talent or interest, or the influence of family background, but you should be careful not to lock yourself into one field too hastily. Flexibility, the capacity to adapt to changing circumstances, may in the end be one of the most desirable characteristics to emerge from any education.

Types of Colleges

COLLEGES come in all sizes and shapes. Your job is to think about what combinations will most encourage your intellectual and personal growth.

Small colleges have traditionally emphasized teaching and close student/faculty relationships. At such colleges, it is not unusual for small seminars to meet in the evening around the fireplace at a professor's home. Where the student/faculty ratio is low, teachers are accessible for extra help and for chats.

Some universities, such as the University of Rochester, pride themselves on the attention paid to their undergraduates, despite the fact that their professors publish regularly. Even full professors teach freshmen. At other universities, much of the teaching of freshmen is done by graduate teaching assistants. There is no reason that a graduate student can't be an exciting teacher; however, if these differences are important to you, check them out carefully.

Some students prefer the diversity, the broad choice of courses, and the social anonymity of a university setting to the more familiar community of the small college. Each has its virtues and its drawbacks. Such considerations boil down to personal taste and need. You may not find it easy to pick four or five colleges that satisfy your criteria and whose admissions standards match your qualifications. There probably is, in fact, no one perfect school or program for you to enroll in. Come as close as you can by making intelligent and thoughtful compromises. Discuss these issues with a counselor, your parents, the college representatives who visit your school, and your campus or alumni interviewers.

Some colleges and all universities offer you the combination of liberal arts study and specialized preprofessional courses. For instance, Skidmore College, although primarily a liberal arts institution, does offer an undergraduate major in business. The University of Rochester and Northwestern University allow undergraduates to take a limited number of courses each year at their graduate business schools. At the University of Pennsylvania, Boston University, the University of California at Los Angeles, Cornell University, and Syracuse University, for instance, an undergraduate could conceivably put together a course of study from the several colleges of arts and sciences, business, or communications that make up the university.

PUBLIC OR PRIVATE COLLEGES

State universities in the United States make up an impressive system of reasonably priced education. About 80% of all college students attend public colleges and universities nationwide.

Families often worry that a public institution may be too big, that the quality of the curriculum or of the student body will not match those of a private college, or that the degree will not have the same value as that from a private institution.

Weighed against these concerns are some definite advantages. A student can move through the state system, starting at a two-year division and moving up to a four-year branch to complete his or her education. The cost is significantly lower. Four years of a private college can run to a minimum of $80,000. A four-year public education, on the other hand, would run closer to $25,000 or $30,000. To attend a prestigious private college, you need to ask yourself, are you and your family willing to incur debt or are you willing to take on work-study?

The size of large state schools may be minimized by seeking out their Honors programs. For instance, the Honors Program at Oswego or Buffalo in the New York State University system would have only about twenty students per class who would also live together in their own residential quarters. Within the University of Michigan's College of Literature, Science, and the Arts is the Residential College, which offers a demanding program within the larger university. Separate from the Residential College, the University offers the Honors Program, open by invitation to about 15% of entering freshmen. At the University of California at Los Angeles, admission to the Honors Collegium is highly competitive; status confers special scholarship eligibility and on-campus housing assistance. At the University of Texas at Austin, about five hundred students out of nearly thirty-four thousand undergraduates qualify for the Plan II liberal arts Honors Program. The University of North Carolina at Chapel Hill's Honors Program invites about two hundred high school seniors to join.

Public universities offer broad menus of courses. Within any state system, however, you need to know where the strong departments are. Some branches are smaller and thus offer seminar-style classes.

There is no question that there is a prestige factor built into attending private colleges and universities, an old-boy or old-girl network as it were that can be helpful to you through an alumni/alumnae network. However, an interesting fact sheds light on the old maxim that it is the individual who makes the degree, not vice versa. Among universities whose M.B.A. programs are consistently ranked among the top twenty, several are public, such as the University of Michigan, Indiana University, and the University of California.

For admission into graduate and professional schools, it is how well you have done academically and on your entrance examinations that counts, more than the prestige of the college you attended. Programs are on the lookout for students who bring diversity through background.

For some of you, attending a local college or university will make you feel more comfortable than going far away and leaving behind family, friends, and Fido all at once. You need to feel ready to make the most out of whatever you choose.

Admissions applications to state universities tend to be less detailed than those for private colleges. Very often no personal essay is required. If you are writing a statement about yourself and your educational goals for private colleges, I recommend that you include that statement with your application to public colleges as well. If it is well done, it can only work to your advantage. Let the admissions committee decide whether or not they want to read it as part of your application. Within a state system there are varying degrees of selectivity among the branches. Some include a more subjective analysis of an application than others, which focus on grade point average and test scores.

If the state system includes several colleges and universities, you are usually allowed to include choices in order of preference on one application form. If not admitted to your first choice, you are likely to be admitted to one of the others or given a choice within the state system.

As a state resident you have a much greater chance of gaining admission to one of your state's universities. The fees for in-state students are considerably lower, since state tax dollars help to support the college. Do be aware that a majority of students from within a state does affect the makeup of the student body and its character. There will not be as much diversity, in all likelihood.

If you are considering applying to a state university outside your own state, keep in mind that you may be part of an out-of-state quota or percentage of admissible applicants, which may be as low as 10% or 15% at some universities. At the University of Connecticut, 87% of the enrolled students are from the state of Connecticut. At the University of Virginia, 63% are in-state. Admissions requirements are also much higher for out-of-state applicants to state universities.

TWO-YEAR COLLEGES

Two-year colleges should not be viewed as last-resort choices for those who cannot get into a four-year college. Junior colleges provide opportunities with unique advantages.

First, they are an excellent way to find direction. Second, tuition and overall costs at two-year colleges are significantly lower than those at four-year colleges. Third, faculty are highly attuned to the needs of individual students. They are hired to teach, not to conduct research, and the classroom is their priority. Fourth, many junior colleges offer a combination of liberal arts courses and highly specialized professional training. Dean Junior College, in Franklin, Massachusetts, for example, offers associate degrees in diverse programs such as Construction Management, Communication Arts, and Child Studies, in addition to Liberal Studies. Although admission to some private two-year colleges can be fairly competitive, these colleges provide an opportunity for students to build creditable academic records and enter four-year schools in their junior year for which they would not have been qualified as high school seniors. Last, an associate degree allows you to obtain work in your field of interest for a year or two with better pay as you test out that interest before you go on to complete a four-year education of specialized study. This last advantage may also be a way to earn money to complete your education.

COOPERATIVE EDUCATION

Some colleges and universities offer a cooperative education plan. A student attends classes full-time for part of the year and works full-time the rest of the year. It usually requires five years to complete a degree on the co-op plan. Annual earnings can average $6,000 or more. In some fields, such as business, job experience is highly valued, which may give a co-op student excellent employment opportunities. The work experience as part of college also lets you know if you like and are good at your intended career.

Some colleges with well-known co-op programs are American University, Antioch College, Baylor University, Drexel University, Kalamazoo College, Northeastern University, Wilberforce University, Wofford College, and Worcester Polytechnic Institute.

THE MILITARY ACADEMIES

Admission to the military academies is competitive and requires nomination by a congressman. Academic standards are high; an average SAT at West Point runs mid 600s in math and mid 500s in verbal. The bachelor of science degree takes four years plus summers to complete, and a student is graduated as a commissioned officer. The federal government pays all costs plus a monthly allowance of around $500. Upon graduation the junior officer must serve a specific length of time, which varies with the particular branch of the service.

The United States military academies are located at

West Point, New York: Army
Annapolis, Maryland: Navy
Colorado Springs, Colorado: Air Force
New London, Connecticut: Coast Guard
Kings Point, New York: Merchant Marine

Alternatives to College

STUDY ABROAD

THERE are many opportunities for study abroad, both as a visiting student for one year or as a degree candidate. We shall consider only a few examples.

The British American Educational Foundation, 1 West 53rd Street, New York, New York, 10019 (212-772-3890), offers an opportunity to study for one year at an English secondary school such as Eton, Winchester, or Harrow. Strong candidates may do this as a thirteenth year or spend two years at a British school before going to an American college. American students who think about studying full-time at a British university are put on nearly equal footing with their British contemporaries by spending a thirteenth year at a British school.

St. Andrews University in Scotland, founded in 1411, attracts and welcomes students from schools and universities all over the world. Overseas undergraduates may elect a full four-year degree program or study for one year before transferring to a home university. Located in a medieval university city, St. Andrews is about one hour by train from Edinburgh.

Richmond College, the American international college in London, attracts students from over seventy countries. It is well known for its unique blend of American and British educational and cultural traditions. Students can study for either a B.A. or associate

(A.A.) degree and may spend a semester, a summer, or one year or more at Richmond.

The American College in Paris, located in central Paris, was founded in 1962 and is accredited in the United States. The College offers a B.A. or B.S. degree with classes taught in English, except for foreign languages and literature. About 50% of the student body is American. Students may be housed with native families. Enrollment is possible as a degree candidate, transfer student, or visiting student. Contact The American College in Paris, 80 East 11th Street, Suite 434, New York, New York, 10003 (212-677-4870).

The International Christian Youth Exchange, 134 West 26th Street, New York, New York, 10001, organizes year-long exchanges to twenty-nine countries for students of all religious backgrounds between the ages of sixteen and eighteen. The program emphasizes social service through volunteer work in hospitals, schools, peace organizations, farms, construction, day-care centers, and social agencies.

EARLY COLLEGE

There are some colleges that offer unique experiences to high school students who qualify to begin college early.

Located in Great Barrington, Massachusetts, Simon's Rock of Bard College is a four-year coeducational liberal arts college designed for high-school-age students. Most students enrolled at Simon's Rock enter after grade ten or eleven and are graduated four years later with a B.A. degree. For over twenty years Simon's Rock has offered students precociously ready for college an opportunity for the increased independence and responsibility beyond the scope of a typical high school curriculum or format. Faculty work closely with students to encourage intellectual growth within a challenging program and personal development with individual support.

The Clarkson School, founded in 1978, is a special division of Clarkson University, in Potsdam, New York, which offers qualified high school juniors a head start on college. Students who have shown excellence in their academic work, especially in math and science, may apply to spend their senior year at the Clarkson School instead of high school. Clarkson School students are housed together in their own dormitory and may use the resources and facilities of Clarkson University. Some exceptional students are admitted before they have completed eleventh grade. This alternative bridge year between high school and college is particularly useful for students interested in careers in engineering, medicine, science, or computers.

WORK EXPERIENCE

An increasing number of students are choosing alternatives to college the year after being graduated from high school. At one time, when seniors spoke of "taking a year off" parents asked cynically, "Off from what?" In recent years parents have become more convinced of the value of having some time in which to think about goals and interests rather than rush off to college before one feels ready.

Alternatives to freshman year are now more commonly accepted as a chance to experience life away from home outside of the classroom setting. They allow a student a chance to step back and do some long-range planning about his or her personal and career objectives.

Such an opportunity is provided by Dynamy, located in Worcester, Massachusetts, an innovative internship program. Dynamy is a year-long educational experience that combines internships with apartment living and outdoor challenge. After this one year, over 90% of Dynamy interns go on to college.

Thirteenth-year experiences lead to the development of independence and increased maturity. We have seen the range of possibilities through some examples discussed earlier, from a homestay program to study at a British school to Dynamy.

A surprisingly high number of college students do not complete their degree at the institution in which they begin it. Too often they pursue college as the thing to do rather than as something they want to do. Caught in the fast track of education, they have met societal and parental expectations without exploring their own inner conflicts about what they would like to do. Some who have never experienced the world of work or reached beyond their own needs to give of their time and expertise to others genuinely benefit from an alternative year. They grow up and actually make for more-promising college applicants, with a different point of view from that of their peers of similar educational backgrounds. Colleges have been highly responsive to the applications of students who have made a thoughtful choice of a thirteenth-year program.

College applications need not be delayed in order to pursue an alternative year. Most private colleges, and some public universities, will grant a formal deferment of one year. This request must be made of an admissions office in writing and should contain a description of what you plan to do. It is technically easier to have an application processed while you are still in high school than to route teacher recommendations, transcripts, and SAT or ACT scores to colleges from a phone or post office in Finland or London. However, some students choose to delay making applications so that what they do and accomplish during the alternative year will make them stronger or more appealing applicants.

Exploring Possibilities

INDEXES, GUIDEBOOKS, AND CATALOGUES

YOU need to consider the best way to begin finding out about colleges and universities without trying to see most of them firsthand.

It makes little sense and a lot of work to send for college catalogues and viewbooks from every college in which you might eventually be interested. Instead, begin hunting by looking through one of the many indexes to colleges, such as *The College Handbook* or a *Peterson's Guide*. The entries, usually organized alphabetically under states, will tell you about the size, location, admission requirements and standards, academic majors offered, and special features, such as learning support services, of each college. Addresses and phone numbers are listed, as are application deadlines and interview and test requirements. Indexes are available from bookstores, in the college guidance office of your high school, or in the reference section of a public library.

Other guidebooks are more subjective, such as *The Insider's Guide to the Colleges* or *The Fiske Guide to Colleges*. These guides give the flavor of each college, with student and faculty comments, descriptions of social life, and mention of particularly strong departments. They are useful supplements to indexes and catalogues.

Some students find computer programs useful. These instruct you to key in your criteria, such as size, location, academic interests, religious affiliation, etc., and then print up a list of appropriate colleges.

Each college also publishes its own catalogue, describing its philosophy, admissions information, and courses. For a more enjoyable overview, you will want to look through the pictorial viewbooks, which contain condensed versions of catalogue information, student comments, and appealing photos of student life. Keep in mind that viewbooks are published with the help of public relations firms at considerable expense to college budgets. They are recruitment tools. They do, however, serve as a pleasant starting point before you invest the time and money to trek off on a college visit. Most colleges will also lend you a video. This will give you a glimpse of campuses and dorms and of students at work and at play. It is also interesting to see in a video what colleges select to show and say about themselves.

THE HIGH SCHOOL COLLEGE COUNSELOR

Begin to visit the counseling office regularly in the second half of your junior year. Do not be afraid to be a "nuisance." The biggest nuisance is for a counselor to feel uninformed of your plans and your concerns.

The high school counselor is your liaison with the colleges. His or her role is not to get you admitted but to help you in the exploration of possibilities and the execution of the application process. He or she can indeed bring the facts about you and your background to a college admissions counselor's attention. Your role is to let your high school counselor know about such things as financial needs, separation or divorce in your family, illness, or anything else that has affected your development and performance in school.

You should discuss your priorities with your high school counselor. If you prefer Pomona to Macalester, say so and why. Take advantage of the books and catalogues in the counseling office. September and October should be months of focused exploration.

Listen for announcements about college visitors to your high school, college nights, local college fairs, local interview or introduction sessions given by colleges, and test registration dates. Be sure you know the deadlines for the SAT, ACT, or Achievement Tests.

THE PARENT CONFERENCE

I strongly recommend at least one conference between the high school college counselor and the family. The student should always be present at these conferences. Of course, not every high school is staffed with a counselor or administration who will have the time to meet with you and your parents on a regular basis. In such cases, you should discuss your plans with your parents and then share them by appointment with your assigned guidance counselor.

Plan ahead for any conference. Arrive with a carefully thought-out list of colleges that you would like to talk about further. Among these might be some you are sure you want to apply to. But be open to new suggestions from the counselor. He or she will know the competition you will face for particular schools.

Eventually, you should narrow your list to four to seven choices, depending upon the level of selectivity. Your final list should include one or two long shots or dream or reach schools where acceptance is possible but not likely, two or three colleges where your chances for acceptance are very good, and two where acceptance is relatively certain.

Discuss with your counselor the pattern of acceptances from your high school to the colleges on your list. Do they tend to accept scholars, only those with high test scores, athletes in certain sports, or children of alumni? Every high school has a certain, established relationship with each college former graduates have applied to in the recent past. That history will have some bearing on your application.

ndent counselor should never be a ghostwriter of your
ather serve as a sounding board to help you evaluate
ences and react to your essay drafts. He or she should
what the different colleges look for in an application
o you about those differences.

ould not consult with an independent counselor under
ression that they will "get you into" a certain college.
of counselors who promise miracles. An effective coun-
orks to empower you to select an appropriate list of schools,
derstand what you have to offer colleges, to help you articulate
contributions, to know what particular colleges look for, and
ome to terms with the technical, personal, and psychological
ponents of the application process. Independent counselors are
guidance and support service.

In general, independent counselors work with a broader base of
colleges and students than do most high school counselors. They
often function well to provide you with a second opinion about
what colleges might work out well for you.

You, not a graduating class, are the primary concern of an
independent counselor. It is his or her main role to work and think
with you about the college application process. They do not teach,
advise clubs, or have multiple school duties. Many students like the
structure that scheduled appointments with a counselor over a
period of time provide to guide them through a complex process.
During other times in our lives that involve change and transition,
we seek help. Why not over the college application process, which
for most of you calls for the most difficult decision-making you
have so far had to engage in? If seeking help makes the process a
productive one in which you learn about yourself and the selection
process, then it is worth it.

Professional services are costly. However, many independent
counselors speak locally at college fairs or as *pro bono* work for
organizations in your area to reach out to a larger community.
Watch for such public appearances on local television or radio

THE INDEPENDENT

Some of you may feel that you
to give you the time and atten.
college application process produ

You will then face the question of
seek the services of an independent c
or her credentials carefully. The best
likely to be someone who has used a cour
attest to his or her care, helpfulness, and
pendent counselors are likely to be member
ciation of College Admissions Counselors
Educational Counselors Association. Each
members.

Independent counselors are in the position of vi
individual more than as a member of a junior or a se
will schedule time as you need it, and work will occur
one basis. The independent counselor's office is a place
the regular schedule and demands of your school. It pr
time and place, a sanctuary if you like, that are strictly yo
explore your ideas, concerns, feelings, and those of your fa
about applying to college.

An effective independent counselor takes the time to get to kno
you well enough to help you evaluate your credentials, qualifications, and experiences for college applications. There are plenty of
stories about some guidance offices that simply show students
Rolodexes of recent applicants from that school, where they applied and were admitted, and what their range of scores and grade
point averages were. Unless your statistics match theirs, you may be
discouraged from trying to gain admission to certain colleges.
Sometimes little thought is given to personal experiences, challenges, or hardships and how they might translate into effective
essays that might make a difference at certain colleges.

programs. College admissions is a hot topic that finds its way into the media with great frequency.

While a professional service will cost your family money, remember that so will driving or flying around the country to look at colleges that may prove totally inappropriate or inaccessible. Time spent with a professional to devise a wise plan of action will save both money and time in the long run.

Choose an independent counselor as carefully and thoughtfully as you would a doctor or therapist. It is very important that he or she be a good listener, with a personality compatible with your own, as well as a highly regarded professional in the field of education.

THE POSTGRADUATE YEAR

If you explore the possibilities we have been discussing and still are not sure you are ready to leave high school but wish to continue your studies, you may want to consider a postgraduate, or PG, year at a private boarding school. This is a costly option, running as high as $18,000 in some cases for the year, but it does allow you to make up course work and build academic credentials. PG sections are kept fairly small so that you receive an appropriate amount of personal attention.

Our society tends to put students on the fast track to college. You need to know that it is okay not to rush into the step if you are not ready. Especially because there is a high cost involved, a PG year will need to be a family decision. For boarding schools with PG programs, consult *Peterson's Guide to Secondary Schools* or *The Handbook of Private Schools*. It is important to check the entry for each or the school's own catalogue to see how large a PG section is. You may feel more comfortable being one of a number of high school graduates completing a thirteenth year and not one of only a handful.

One fallacy is that the PG year will springboard you into Harvard or Stanford or another top-flight school. It *may* do that, but your motive in doing a PG year should not wholly be based on that hope or assumption. You may well enhance your credentials during that year and that will indeed make you more attractive to selective colleges. But do not invest the money and time in a PG year with only that one goal of getting into Stanford in mind, or at the end of yet one more year of high school you will feel sorely disillusioned if that expectation is not met.

You may want to include one or two PG programs among your list of college applications. If you do not get accepted into a college you want to attend, you may prefer the PG year.

PART TWO

Getting There

The College Application

W HEN you think about sitting down and filling out an application to college, a simple set of blank lines and boxes can suddenly look very threatening. Why? For one thing, College X, which has been only a name, starts to become a real possibility, a place where you might live and study. Going to college becomes more of a reality. You wonder if your credentials and accomplishments will be impressive enough. What if there are five lines for activities and you have only four things to list? The application forms become documents by which you will be at least partially judged. And to some extent this is true. You wonder, "What are THEY really looking for in asking that question?" "Is an optional essay really optional or are they looking to see who answers it and who doesn't?" "Does it matter if I list an intended major or just check 'undecided'? Will they think I can't make up my mind?"

I recommend that about halfway through your junior year, when you prepare for the time when you will begin filling out applications, you ask your school registrar or adviser for a copy of your high school transcript. Often when I ask students to recall their grades, they remember selectively; a C in English is remembered as a C+. One of my favorite anecdotes about the college application process is the classic story about the young man who eagerly approached his school counselor to express his wish to attend Princeton. "Mr. Tolls," the surprised counselor replied, "are you aware that you are in the bottom half of your class?" "Oh," gasped Mr. Tolls, "I knew I wasn't in the top half, but I didn't realize I was in the bottom."

Look at your transcript and you will see what colleges are going to see. You still have time in the first half of senior year to make up for some lost ground by selecting courses thoughtfully and doing well. You also have the summer after junior year to consider some of the alternatives we have discussed on pp. 14–16, which might strengthen your profile.

For most of you a college application is the most complex set of forms you have ever filled out. The concerns and fears you feel as you approach that stack of papers are understandable. Not much in our schooling teaches us how to fill out such forms.

Filing applications comes in the first half of senior year, as you are trying to keep grades high, prepare for standardized testing if you have not completed it, continue your commitments to sports and clubs, tutor the kids at the neighborhood community center, and have some kind of social life. This is not an easy balancing act.

Then, there are Mom and Dad, who want to be helpful, and they construct a weekly schedule for you to adhere to so that all applications will be out before Thanksgiving. If you read the section on parents, I think you will better understand some of the reasons why parents often overidentify with their children, especially during the application process, and why you have such mixed or ambivalent feelings about their involvement.

For complicated reasons, some of them psychological, a set of application forms can become a threat, a source of confusion and anxiety. A college application asks you to look at yourself. You are forced, in a way, to evaluate your achievements and accomplishments and to come to terms with your limitations. If you have not achieved a position of leadership, received academic accolades, or had an important effect on the lives of others, there is little chance to do so in the month before these forms have to be mailed. There is also a way in which in filling out an application you are on your way toward making a commitment to go to college. The application is the first step of a contract, if you like, between you and a school, and it is an agreement between you and your parents and with yourself that you are about to move on.

Is it any wonder that a college application assumes so much importance in the mind of someone filling one out for the first time?

Once you become aware of some of the reasons why completing a college application can seem so difficult, you are on your way to doing it well.

To obtain applications, call the admissions office or send a postcard or note with a request like the one below.

I am in my senior year at _____ School in __(City or Town, State)__ and am interested in applying for admission to __(Name of college)__ for the fall of 19_____. I plan to pursue a program in __(liberal arts, science, business, etc.).__ Please send me an application, catalogue, and any other admission information.

Thank you.

Sincerely yours,
(Name) _____
(Address) _____

Many colleges open a file on you as soon as they receive such a request.

Most applications will ask you to record your social security number. If you don't already have one, you should obtain one before getting too far along in the application process. Other forms, such as the SAT registration, will also request a social security number. In the computer age, information is brought up onto a computer screen when you call an admissions office about your candidacy.

You will also be required to have a social security number if you and your family apply for financial aid. It is advisable, then, to obtain one before midway through your junior year in high school.

I urge you to view the applications, especially the essays, as a chance to express yourself. This is your opportunity to go beyond the numbers of standardized test scores and grades. Some of the best advice I have heard comes from the admissions director at the University of Chicago, Theodore A. O'Neill, who urges applicants to view the application as a conversation or dialogue between themselves and the admissions committee. This is your opportunity to present yourself—the only chance some of you will have unless you go for a personal interview. You cannot get away from the fact that you are going to be judged; after all, a decisive judgment has to be reached at the end of the process about whether or not to admit you. The response to every question does have a consequence, which is why filling out an application needs to be taken seriously.

O'Neill encourages students to think of an application as their chance to tell their own story. You are like a character in a novel. Admissions readers want to understand who you are, what your capacities are, and what you want to do at their college and in the years beyond.

THE PARTS OF AN APPLICATION

Let's consider the different parts of a typical college application form.

Most applications are made up of the following:

- a Personal Section. You are asked to give your name and address and other statistical information about your family, your educational background, your standardized testing, work experience, activities, academic interests, and one or more essay topics.
- Faculty Recommendation Forms.
- a Secondary School Counselor Form.
- Financial Aid Forms. These are to be filled out in addition to the Financial Aid Form of the College Scholarship Service.

As an application continues, the questions become increasingly personal. You have to begin to think about such things as possible fields of academic concentration, possible career plans, standardized testing plans, academic distinctions, and the activities to which you have committed your time. You will need to consider what these interests have meant to you and why and perhaps why you are applying to a specific college.

The activities section on most application forms looks something like the one on the following page.*

When you list items remember to be specific. If you have been captain of a team, co-editor of the literary magazine, or class representative to the student government, say so, don't just list soccer or lit mag. Specify if the team was junior varsity or varsity. This is your chance to personalize the activities section. If one or two of your activities need further explanation, feel free to write a brief paragraph about them on an extra sheet. Say, for instance, that you were instrumental in reviving a moribund debate team, or that you had to gain support from a parents' association group to get it funded and personally set up the first year's debate schedule against other teams. That would be worth telling, in an extra paragraph or in the space for an optional essay about yourself. Just put an asterisk next to that entry on the activity grid and write "Please see attached sheet" and a reader will know you have more to tell.

Where you are asked to comment on or list travel experiences, be careful not to put together what is nothing more than an itinerary. Travel in itself, without some educational component, has little bearing on college admissions. It simply does not tell much about you. That educational component need not be a class; it might be keeping a daily journal, doing some photography, or living with a foreign family for a while to concentrate on improving your fluency in their language. It is how you view any journey that makes it of interest to an admissions committee. Some students tour the Far

* Taken from the Common Application; see pp. 65–66.

EXTRACURRICULAR AND PERSONAL ACTIVITIES

Please list your principal extracurricular, community, and family activities and hobbies in the order of their interest to you. Include specific events and/or major accomplishments such as musical instrument played, varsity letters earned, etc. Please (✔) in the right column those activities you hope to pursue in college.

Activity	Grade level or post-secondary (p.s.) 9 10 11 12 P.S.	Approximate time spent — Hours per week	Weeks per year	Positions held, honors won, or letters earned	Do you plan to participate in college?

East and are so little able to reflect on the experience that it seems to have had little impact on them. Others can make a trip near their home vitally interesting because they discover something important in the familiar. Rather than merely listing foreign countries under activities, unless there is a separate area for travel, it is preferable to discuss the opportunity and importance of travel in an interview or essay.

Applications are, among other things, a way for the college to see if you can follow directions.

Some directions specify that you contain your responses to "the space below." Some give you permission to attach extra sheets if you exceed the given space. Some ask that you begin a written or typed response in the given space and then continue on separate sheets. On other forms, it is acceptable to print "Please see attached essay" and include it on separate sheets.

Do whatever the directions say to do. Brown University, for example, has for many years required that the personal essay be printed or written out in longhand, not typed.

If you print any application by hand, use black or dark blue ink, not Day-Glo green. Readers have to look at thousands of these forms, and black or blue ink is easiest on the eyes.

If you make corrections, erase neatly or use white-out fluid sparingly, not in blobs.

Before you print or type any information on the actual application form, you should photocopy the form and practice on it. This allows you to see how much writing will fit into the given space. You can edit without spoiling the original copy.

As you begin to send for applications, it is a good idea to make a checklist like the one suggested on p. 64 to keep a record of application deadlines and other information.

Many colleges will send you a card acknowledging that they have received your application. It is a good idea to record that receipt on the chart. Once you feel that there has been time for all your credentials, including teacher recommendations, to

College	Campus Visit	Application Sent for	Application Received	Interview	Application Deadline	Scores Sent

have reached the admissions office, call to make sure that your application is considered complete.

A canceled check for the application fee is proof that a college has received and acknowledged your application.

Keep a photocopy of everything that you send to colleges. In the event that something is lost, you won't need to do it over.

When you speak to an admissions counselor or secretary, keep a record of the phone conversation with the date and the person's name. You may need to refer to this later and be unable to recall the information without such a record.

Most colleges require that SAT, ACT, and Achievement Test results arrive officially from the test services, the Educational Testing Service (ETS) or the American College Testing Service (ACT). Scores can be requested at the time of registration for the tests or later by telephone or by a written request form called the Additional Report Form, obtainable from your high school guidance or counseling office. High schools in most cases do record test scores on the official transcript, but colleges do not consider these reports official.

An official score report presents a cumulative picture of the examinations you have taken and the scores you have received on them. You cannot delete a result once the examination has been scored. Therefore, if you take the SAT twice, each set of scores will appear on the printout you receive or request be sent to colleges after the second test.

THE COMMON APPLICATION

Well over one hundred colleges have agreed to accept a form called the Common Application. These are available from a high school or independent counselor. Instead of completing a form for each individual college, you may photocopy this Common Application and send it to any member of the group. Those colleges who participate are listed on the cover of the Common Application. Its format is the same as that mentioned earlier.

A frequent question about the Common Application is "Will it hurt my chances if I use it?" This is a difficult question to answer with certainty. The form states: "No distinction will be made between the Common form and the college's own form." Some colleges do use two different forms, their own and the Common. Where this is the case, check to see how they differ. Some college application forms are more individualized and contain essay questions beyond the standard topics that appear on the Common Application. Where there are extra essays, I believe you should answer them, even if you choose to use the Common form. In other words, use it, but don't take any shortcuts. If you have doubts about using the Common Application, ask the admissions representative who visits your high school or attends a college fair how they regard the Common Application. Or you can always call the admissions office itself to ask.

A few offices have said that they do not mind the Common's being used in an emergency, but that they prefer you to use their own under normal circumstances. I believe that most of the colleges listed on the Common Application permit you to use it without jeopardy, but you should opt to use the Common Application only if you feel comfortable using it.

THE TEACHER EVALUATION FORM

Teacher evaluations are an important part of most applications.

This form is given to a teacher who knows you well and who will be required to fill out three main parts. The first is a short response section with questions such as "How long have you known this student?" or "What words come to mind to describe this student?" A second section asks for a written evaluation, a description of the student's motivation, independence, intellectual curiosity, and other academic and personal characteristics. Other questions are among the following:

Give evidence about the nature of this applicant's motivation for academic work, the breadth and depth of intellectual interests, the originality, independence, sensitivity, and power of the applicant's mind, and the applicant's capacity for growth. Is he or she, for instance, excessively grade-conscious or driven by family pressure?

To what extent has he or she been genuinely interested in academic work and made full use of intellectual potential?

What are your impressions of the applicant's character, aims, and values? How do fellow students, other teachers, and you regard him or her as a person compared with his or her contemporaries?

Does the applicant have any special strengths, weaknesses, or problems of which we should be aware?

What is the quality of the applicant's performance in extracurricular, community, or work activity? Does he or she have any unusual competence, talent, or capacity for leadership?

Is this student self-directed? Is he or she studying for personal satisfaction or for grades?

Does this student pursue studies beyond assignments, or does he or she have to be prodded?

Are there ways in which this applicant has distinguished himself or herself in your class?

A third section is usually a grid like the one following, taken from the Common Application.

You should give your teacher evaluation forms (some colleges request two) to teachers who know you and your work well. Generally, you are expected to seek out teachers who have taught you in grades eleven or twelve. In some cases, your special achievement in a tenth-grade class might qualify the teacher of that class to write about the importance of that exercise to you, but in most cases ninth- and tenth-grade teachers are unable to comment about your current motivation and readiness to take on college-level work.

Some colleges require only one teacher evaluation form; others require two. With private colleges, it is always okay to photocopy the form and ask a second evaluator to send one, too. If you choose your two teachers wisely, each might show a different and important side of you. Taken together, a recommendation from a science

RATINGS

Compared to other college-bound students whom you have taught, check how you would rate this student in terms of academic skills and potential:

	No basis	Below Average	Average	Good (above average)	Very Good (well above average)	Excellent (top 10%)	One of the top few encountered in my career
Creative, original thought							
Motivation							
Independence, initiative							
Intellectual ability							
Academic achievement							
Written expression of ideas							
Effective class discussion							
Disciplined work habits							
Potential for growth							
SUMMARY EVALUATION							

teacher and one from an English teacher might provide more perspective on you than either one alone.

How should you request a recommendation from a teacher?

Start by making a formal appointment to discuss the request for a recommendation. Too often students fail to plan ahead and right before deadlines accost a teacher in a crowded hallway and jam six recommendation forms into his or her hands. Listen for a growl.

Most teachers are flattered by your request for support. In every high school, however, there are certain junior-year and senior-year teachers who are deluged each fall with recommendation requests because they have earned a reputation for doing recommendations with sensitivity and thoroughness. They know their students' work habits and intellectual capabilities and have a keen knowledge of what will be helpful to a college reader. Teachers receive no extra compensation for writing letters of recommendation. It is a painstaking task that must be done on top of preparing assignments and grading papers. You are not entitled to a recommendation; that is something you earn over time.

Before you ask for a recommendation, discuss with the teacher how favorably or strongly he or she feels your candidacy can be honestly supported. If a teacher cannot be an enthusiastic supporter, a refusal is kinder than a lukewarm or highly qualified statement.

Share your goals with the teacher, review your work for that course, your interests in school and out, and your choice of colleges. Provide a set of stamped envelopes with addresses of college admissions offices clearly written or typed. You should ask the same teacher to send his or her letter to each college. An exception to this would be a letter of recommendation from a teacher who is an alumnus or alumna of a college to which you are applying.

The teacher should photocopy his or her letter, in case you add a college later. Most teachers do not write completely different letters for each college. They copy their letter and attach it to the form for the teacher evaluation. They may well choose to vary the checkmarks on the grid, believing that you are more qualified for one college over another, and so check "very good" for highly competitive College X and "excellent" for less competitive College Z.

The only control you have over a faculty recommendation is the judgment you use in selecting the teachers. The most effective recommendations are those written with confidentiality. Under the Family Educational Rights and Privacy Act of 1974, it is your legal right to see your recommendations once you are enrolled in a college. A waiver of this right appears on many applications. Many students ask whether to waive their rights to see their recommendations. I can only offer my opinion, not tell you what to decide. I believe you should ask no person to write for you whose judgment you do not trust or whose opinion you do not value. Most recommendations I have seen tend to be overly complimentary, if they err in any direction.

Many teachers will offer to share their letters with you. They want you to feel reassured and at ease that they have done their best for you. You will be pleasantly surprised at how positive most will sound. You may also marvel at how observant and concerned for your development as a student and a person most teachers have been. Sitting down and sharing your thoughts after a course has been completed can be a valuable as well as an educational experience.

Not signing the waiver does not jeopardize your admission chances. I do believe, however, that you show a vote of confidence in the people you have asked to recommend you by doing so.

When selecting teachers to recommend you, keep the following points in mind:

1. Ask teachers who have taught you recently.
2. Consider asking a teacher whom you have had for more than one class. Such a teacher's evaluation can be illuminating because he or she can discuss your progress and development over the years.
3. Don't necessarily aim for the teacher who has been your

friend. An emotionally detached recommendation may be stronger and more effective.

4. Try to get variety in your recommendations—for instance, one from an English teacher and one from a math teacher, rather than two from English teachers.

5. Select your recommendations to fit your interest. It makes sense to have a science teacher's recommendations among your letters to a premed program.

6. If you have studied under teachers who have contacts at certain college departments, you may want to seek out their recommendations, as they could be influential.

7. Don't necessarily ask teachers in whose courses you have earned A's. On the other hand, a teacher whose course you failed can hardly attest to your academic ability. There is much to be said about the student who tried hard, however; a teacher can speak about your attitude, cooperation, sense of humor, promise, or class participation in addition to your grade in the class.

8. Students often think that a recommendation from the chairman of a department carries more weight than one from a faculty member. This is not necessarily true. It depends upon how thoroughly the teacher or chairman knows your work and you.

The following example of a teacher recommendation demonstrates how effective a letter can be when the teacher is knowledgeable about the student and can use anecdotes and details to back up generalizations. Notice how the recommendation covers classroom performance, the quality of the student's thinking, and her impact on the activities to which she has committed herself.

Susanne Ambers
  There is in Susanne something of the curiosity, the wanderlust, the courage of the pioneers of the country who packed their belongings into covered wagons and set off for new territories. Her rich and

warm personality with all its contours and surprises could have creatively communicated with unknown Indians, forded challenging rivers, and domesticated hostile landscapes. Susanne is equally at home in the sophisticated and competitive environment of her school and of Washington, D.C. She is a favored friend among her peers, a tennis player of distinction, and a serious student. In all of these endeavors, Susanne has the courage of her convictions, the capacity to take risks, and the resilience of our country's settlers.

Susanne takes her academic work seriously not so much because she wants good grades but more because she really wants to understand the world and her place in it. She listens to the discussions around her, never hesitating to add her own insights or ask questions. What I especially admire about Susanne's enthusiasm for learning is that she is completely non-discriminatory in her approach. Whether a student or a teacher, an underclassman, or a peer, is speaking, Susanne will attend to their words and respond with care and consideration. Her respect for the ideas of others and her integrity in her subsequent comments combine to make her a glorious member of a seminar or discussion group.

Many of these skills with words find a solid home in her writing. Susanne is adept at observing the details of behavioral descriptions and environmental situations, and she can interweave these details so that plot and character come alive in her short stories and personality analyses. Her lively imagination allows her to give symbolic depth to her descriptions through twists and turns of narrative that are complex but always believable.

These abilities in expressive and creative writing are matched by Susanne's success in expository and analytical essay writing. She can attack an intricate, dense text and patiently work through the sentences to uncover the core of the piece and then find a clear, sparkling way to communicate its meaning. In a recent essay Susanne composed in response to a computer scientist's essay on the computer's capacity for "thinkinghood," Susanne first presented a flawless outline of his argument and then creatively attacked the premises of the piece. She focused on the complex intertwining of cognition and emotion that form the foundation of the most signifi-

cant contributions to understanding human nature, thereby supporting her criticism of the work.

Susanne balances her academic work with participation in a multitude of activities both in and out of school. She is an active member of both the Harvard and Princeton Model Congress teams and has been for two years. One bill written last year to argue for support for the homeless was particularly well researched and passionately written. Last year Susanne worked with a group of upper school students to introduce a model congress to eighth grade students and was wonderfully successful.

Any extra time Susanne has is spent on the tennis court. She has competed for three years and is nationally ranked. She is a tenacious, energetic, and skillful player, motivated to win while being a gracious good sport.

Susanne has spent much time perfecting her knowledge of modern Greek and French. In Greece and in the south of France, she has immersed herself in the culture and local color of the place and absorbed its mood and thought as well as its language.

Susanne is a student who will be truly missed by her peers and teachers as she moves on to the challenges of college. Perhaps her teachers will miss her more, though, because Susanne is a student who learns the old-fashioned way (paraphrasing John Houseman) — she works at it. And this is the kind of student teachers value most.

THE SECONDARY SCHOOL FORM OR COUNSELOR RECOMMENDATION

Another important part of every application is the Secondary School Form, sometimes referred to as the Counselor Recommendation. Make an appointment with a counselor to discuss your goals and requests. Such discussions, although part of a business meeting, give the counselor a chance to get to know you better. It is important that you make your plans together. You may not necessarily agree on what colleges are best for you or which are attainable; it is important, however, that you get a sense of how supportive your high school counselor feels about your getting into college.

High school counselors are asked to fill out a grid much like that on the teacher evaluation form and to write about you. Many counselors rely on the input they receive from your junior-year teachers. Many high schools have a formal procedure that requests junior-year teachers to submit short evaluations (at the end of the year) on each student they teach. A counselor's evaluation may vary from a few sentences to a two-page essay. This depends in part on the policy of the high school and the size of the senior class. If this seems unfair, that one applicant may have more going for him in a recommendation, rest assured that colleges are familiar with the different counseling styles among high schools. They do not expect as much detailed information from the counselor of a large public high school responsible for advising three hundred students as from a private school counselor advising forty-eight. If you are not at a high school where there is a lot of personal interaction and support between you and a counselor, you will need to assume more responsibility for establishing a relationship with a college representative, your interviewer, a senior teacher, or an independent counselor.

This is a complex and sometimes confusing process. There is no reason you should go through it without support and reassurance.

When all is said and done, the most effective recommendations will come from those who know you well, whether they are famous or unknown to the world at large. Good recommendations contain specific examples, anecdotes, and details. They should say what is special about you and why you are a good match for the college.

NONACADEMIC RECOMMENDATIONS

Although there are no printed forms for outside recommendations in most application packets, it is often a good idea to supplement your academic references with one, perhaps two nonacademic evaluations. These should be chosen with great care and discretion. Do not overcrowd your application folder.

Coaches

If you have excelled at a sport, have your high school coach or private instructor comment on your level of ability and competitiveness. Coaches have a strong network among themselves. College coaches and high school coaches keep in touch, especially if a high school has sent valuable players to the college over the years. Consult your coach about whether you would qualify to play a particular sport at a particular college. If a college has a division team is it Division I, II, or III?

In most cases, athletic ability does not get an otherwise unqualified candidate in. In combination with statistics, personal qualities, and variables such as what part of the country you come from, athletic talent can certainly help draw attention to your application. It also depends on what position needs to be filled the year you apply. If your competitive ability is exceptional, a college coach can, at certain schools, become highly instrumental in getting you noticed by an admissions committee, providing your credentials are in the ballpark.

A word of caution. Some student athletes make the mistake of bypassing high school counselors and high school coaches and start negotiating directly with college coaches. At most colleges, admission is the domain of the admissions office, not the athletic department. You will increase the chances of everyone's working on your behalf if you keep them apprised of your actions. Keeping everyone informed and sharing information allows those involved to coordinate their efforts.

Alumni

Alumni are useful sources of recommendations, especially if they have remained active with their college and stayed in touch with current admissions practices.

Recommendations from big donors—"heavy hitters" as they are called—can carry weight at some colleges more than at others. While this may seem unfair, it is a part of how the real world works. Colleges have to honor the long-standing loyalty and financial support that keeps their endowments healthy. This is one of many variables, along with special talent, geographical distribution, minority status, or alumni legacy, that factor into the composition of a freshman class. Very, very seldom does a totally unqualified applicant get admitted because of a connection with a famous or influential person. Such a recommendation in a folder is more likely to smooth the way for a highly qualified candidate or boost a marginal candidate. *

Be very delicate about whose intervention you solicit. Be sure you trust their style with admissions people, who understandably do not appreciate being badgered on behalf of an applicant.

Peer References

Some colleges, such as Williams and Wesleyan, require that you ask a friend to submit a letter of reference. Choose a friend who both knows you well and knows how to write. Since most teenagers have not written recommendations, they may feel unsure about what to include. You might suggest that your friend share what he or she has written with a teacher or counselor for advice.

---

* "Connections" are people who are thought to be able to make anything happen because they are wealthy, famous, or active alumni and big donors to capital campaigns. I have seen such connections make a difference in about 2% of the thousands of cases I have worked with over fifteen years.

Employers, Supervisors, Clergymen

Anyone who can vouch for the difference you have made to a job or an organization, such as a religious youth group, a tutoring or volunteer program, or a camp, could contribute a valuable optional recommendation, which should in part be a character reference. People who have observed your work with others outside a classroom can describe how your presence significantly changed the group you were a part of or the lives of those you affected.

The College Admissions Office

W E speak of "college admissions." It is important that you understand what a college admissions office is, how an admissions committee works, and what they look for among their applicants.

Admitting students to college is a full-time job done by professionals who make up an admissions committee. Most admissions offices are headed by a dean or a director of admissions who is assisted by associates, assistants, and counselors. Some offices use current college seniors to assist with interviewing. Most now use alumni extensively to conduct interviews regionally. It is also common practice for faculty to sit in committee as voting members on a rotating basis.

Alumni delegated to represent colleges in towns and cities across the country are trained for this task, in most cases, in on-campus workshops. They are not voting committee members, but their write-ups are considered carefully as part of an applicant's folder.

Each admissions counselor is assigned specific parts of the country. It is his or her particular responsibility to know well the high schools in that area, to visit many of them, and to keep up with curriculum and grading practices so as to be a knowledgeable interpreter of that high school's transcripts.

Once your folder is complete, your application will be reviewed by a "first reader." Colleges vary in the number of readers who evaluate an individual application. At Bates College in Lewiston, Maine, for instance, each application is reviewed by four to six readers. Usually, two or three readers read and rank each application before it is discussed or considered by a full committee. At other colleges, a full committee reads only those folders not clearly classified as Admit or Deny.

Colleges use a rating system, which differs from school to school, to evaluate applicants on categories such as academic achievement (which would include the strength of the curriculum, grade point average, and standardized tests), writing ability, personal accomplishment (which would include extracurricular activities and work experience), and service to others.

What do admissions committees look for in an applicant? The committee's responsibility is to attract and admit a diverse, interesting, academically able class consistent with the standards and philosophy of the particular college.

Colleges look to see how you have used your time and what you have made of the opportunities you have had, academic and personal. Smaller colleges are particularly prone to look beyond your classroom performance to see how you have demonstrated leadership, made commitments to activities, and reached out to others.

Kent Jones, director of admissions at Skidmore College, in summing up his admissions committee's objectives, presents a comprehensive picture of what most private colleges look for when reviewing an applicant's file:

> *Above all else, Skidmore seeks students who demonstrate intellectual curiosity and an energetic commitment to learning. Our primary emphasis is on the academic record, and we carefully evaluate the breadth and depth of the secondary school program, the quality of achievement in that program, and the quality of engagement not only in learning but in a student's life beyond the classroom. We rely quite heavily on sources such as the guidance counselor and teacher recommendations, the interview report, the application and application essay to supplement the information available to us on the high school transcript. These additional sources of information about a candidate can be critical and can help us identify those students who are open-minded, who show evidence of integrity, initiative, and a concern for others, and who, by their attitude toward life*

beyond the classroom as well as toward learning, suggest a quality of "engagement" that indicates a readiness and an eagerness to take advantage of a residential liberal arts college such as Skidmore. We play close attention to these additional criteria because we value students who will contribute to the life of the community in varied and exciting ways.

Most colleges admit more students than they can accommodate as enrolled freshmen. Colleges can tell, within a range, what their yield rate is likely to be, that is, how many students admitted will actually enroll. Colleges such as Harvard have high yield rates of around 70%.

Colleges use Wait Lists (discussed on pp. 124–25) to protect against having too few enrolled students.

ADMISSIONS ALTERNATIVES

Several application alternatives are available, depending upon the colleges to which you choose to apply.

Regular Admission

The student submits the application by the deadline published in the college catalogue or handbook and is informed of the admissions decision in April.

Deadlines for regular admissions vary considerably; you will find each college's listed in its literature, under admissions requirements and deadlines. Some deadlines fall as early as December, others as late as February or March. Not all colleges have specific deadlines, but don't procrastinate, as spaces fill up and you limit your admission chances by delaying.

In addition to its regular admission program, Bard College has an innovative Immediate Decision Plan. A student sends for the application papers and informs Bard of his or her intention to apply under this plan, and a time is set for a day session. The student brings the application, transcript, recommendations, and a writing sample to this on-campus session. While the applicant attends a morning seminar, for which he has received an advance reading assignment (participation in this seminar is not a factor in the admissions decision), the admissions team reviews the candidate's credentials. Following the seminar, the candidate participates in three hours of interviews. The committee then tells the student if he or she has been accepted, and if not, why.

Early Decision

If you are sure that you like a particular college above all others, and if your academic record is strong, you should consider applying for Early Decision, provided, of course, that the college you prefer offers such a plan. An Early Decision applicant applies by a certain date and is usually given a decision before December 20. If accepted, you must withdraw any other applications and attend this college. This agreement is made contractually between you and the college when you sign the application for Early Decision status.

Students frequently ask if they increase their chances of admission by applying for Early Decision. At some colleges, the answer is yes. Some selective private colleges admit as many as one-quarter to one-third of their freshman class on Early Decision. An Early Decision application does indicate the seriousness of your interest in a particular college. You do join a group of highly qualified students when you join an Early Decision pool. If there is something attractive about your application, your early interest may tip the scale in your favor, even if you are a marginal candidate. If your credentials are not impressive enough at that time, the admissions committee may suggest specific ways for you to increase your chances by April. For instance, raising your grade in physics to a B+ might give you the edge you need. Having read over your application, the committee can tell you where you are weak and whether or not you can improve enough by April. Sometimes, this extra time allows you to conduct a special project to show the depth of your interest in a subject or activity—directing a student drama production, for example. Work through your counselor and try to discover what your chances will be later and what you might do to improve them.

So long as you love the college, you cannot lose by an Early Decision application. If the college defers you, when you reenter the pool of regular applicants your commitment to that college will work in your favor. If they deny you, and a few colleges do deny on Early, you may as well know sooner rather than later of their lack of interest and turn your attention elsewhere.

You should take the commitment to Early Decision seriously. You may not apply to more than one college Early Decision, and you are agreeing to attend if admitted. Do not try to manipulate the system, as such action is unethical and you are also very likely to be found out in this age of computers.

Early Action

This option is offered to you by Brown, Harvard, Princeton, Yale, and MIT. A few other colleges, such as Tulane and Northwestern, have their own versions of Early Action, but technically speaking, the Ivies listed above and MIT were the originators of this concept.

For Early Action you apply by November 1 or 15 and are informed of a decision by mid-December. If admitted, you need not reply before May 1. Until that date, the college must reserve a place for you in their freshman class. Early Action, in other words, unlike Early Decision, does not require a commitment on your part to attend until May 1.

I recommend Early Action to those whose superior credentials qualify them for highly selective colleges.

Open Admissions

Some colleges admit all students who apply. You do not always get your first choice under this plan, but you are granted entrance to

one college within your state or city system. At City University of New York, the applicant lists six choices that he would be willing to attend within the system. The Admissions Office admits you to the division for which you are best qualified.

Rolling Admission

Those colleges that offer this plan notify you of their decision about four weeks after reviewing your completed application. Some colleges with Rolling Admission do list a preferred deadline if housing is desired on campus.

Deferred Admission

Some students choose to defer entrance into college for one year. They may plan to work to earn money, travel, or pursue a special program in an area of interest. This must be arranged between college and admitted student. The college does have the right to approve or disapprove of the plan under consideration. The student usually may not attend another college during this year except by special arrangement with the college to which he or she has been admitted.

If you are considering a deferment option, I recommend tha you still apply to colleges when you are a high school senic Faculty recommendations will be harder to gather a year later. you can, ask a teacher to write your recommendation and put it file for use at a later date. It is also easier to collect transcripts test scores while in high school than from abroad or if you ar of your home state. Plans also change. By May, a plan you h mind could have fallen through, and you might wish to college after all.

Most colleges are cooperative about deferment, if your tive plan has merit. You will most likely have to pay a deposit to reserve a space in the class for the following y

FACTORS BEYOND YOUR CONTROL

Much of this book is devoted to a discussion of how you can increase your chances for acceptance by knowing what to expect so that by the middle of senior year you will be in a strong position when you apply.

It is also important to realize that some factors which figure importantly in the college's decision are decidedly beyond your control. The kind of high school you have attended—public, private, or parochial—where you come from, your alumni relationships, whether you are a legacy, your minority status, and sports or musical or acting talent, each will affect your chances for admission to a particular college.

It is the objective of every admissions committee to assemble the most impressive freshman class from each year's pool of applicants. The class should reflect diversity of background, talent and interests, intellectual curiosity, and ability appropriate to the standards of the college. Many people think that colleges look for well-rounded students; in fact, they look for a well-rounded class, made up of individuals with distinct characteristics or ability. If the school orchestra has lost its tuba player in June's graduating class, then a tuba-playing B+ student will most likely have an advantage over a non-tuba-playing B+ student, all other considerations being about equal.

Every college puts together a profile of statistics that reflect the composition of its most recent freshman class. These profiles are often in high school guidance offices or are available upon request from some admissions offices. A profile contains information such as the following:

- the number of students accepted who ranked in the top half or quarter of their graduating class
- the number from each level of SAT or ACT and Achievement Test scores

- median SAT or ACT and Achievement Test scores in each subject
- geographical distribution
- admissions figures for specific fields, such as nursing, pre-med, or liberal arts
- the number of applicants and percentages of applicants accepted from public and private schools
- Early Decision admission figures
- alumni children admission figures
- choice of academic major
- athletic ability

Geographical Distribution

Where you come from can either help or hinder your chances of being admitted. Any college strives for representation from the various states and foreign countries. The private colleges have more flexibility than state-supported colleges, which must choose heavily from among state residents who apply. Catalogues and entries in college indexes indicate out-of-state and in-state percentages.

Applying to a private college from a distant state, other factors being equal, could well put the odds on your side. Colleges in the East put enormous effort, for instance, into recruiting qualified candidates from states in the Midwest, West, and Southwest, such as Indiana or Idaho or New Mexico. Geographical distribution is a valued means of achieving on campuses the diversity of background and experience that enriches the college. On the other hand, students from Eastern college preparatory high schools who apply to selective colleges in the East will find it very difficult to distinguish their candidacies from other highly qualified Eastern applicants to these same Eastern colleges.

Alumni Children, "Legacies"

Being the child of a graduate of a particular college definitely increases your chances for acceptance. Colleges like to establish the loyalty that comes with family tradition. Such loyalty not only makes for a close supportive community and personal service to the college, it tends to yield generous donations over time to maintain standards and facilities and strong faculties. Kenyon College, for instance, admitted about 60% of those alumni children who applied to the class of 1989. Children of alumni/alumnae make up about 10%–12% of Stanford University's freshman class each year and are accepted at close to double the rate of non-legacies. The University of Pennsylvania accepts about 58% of all legacy applicants.

Minority Status

Colleges actively seek minority students who will add strength and diversity to their communities. Minority applicants need to look carefully at campus communities. There is an important difference between recruiting and admitting minority applicants and serving their needs with sensitivity. Is there a significant minority population in the college or the larger community around it among which you will be comfortable? Does this matter to you? Is there personal support if you want or need it? Don't let the prestige factor and the flattery of being recruited lure you into a mismatch. In the long run, getting in will not be as important as being happy and successful wherever you go.

Choice of Academic Major

Your major may affect your chances for admission at some colleges. For example, premed is highly competitive; colleges do not want to accept candidates who are likely to have great difficulty getting into medical school four years later. You should not apply for a premed program unless you have proven ability in math and science and an excellent overall record and high standardized test scores.

Universities famous for their medical schools, such as the University of Pennsylvania, Johns Hopkins, Stanford, Duke, the University of Chicago, and the University of Rochester among others, are particularly sensitive to their liberal arts reputation on the undergraduate level. The philosophy department at Hopkins, for instance, happens to be first-rate. A bright non-premed would stand a good chance of being admitted, whereas the bright premed has to be exceptional to meet the challenge of the competition. Do not enter a university as an English major with the intention of switching to premed or declare a science major when you really want premed (these cases are referred to as closet premeds!). Switching to premed is not easy; it requires very high grades and a proven track record in math and science and perhaps even some summer makeup work.

Students who have an interest in majoring in the classics—Greek and Latin—often rise above the competition for places in some of the Ivies or at small private colleges, where classics departments are looking for potential majors. Such colleges recognize the importance of these departments to a traditional liberal arts education and carefully seek students to study in them.

Students interested in the possibility of a career in education are valued applicants. Such declarations should be backed up with experience as a tutor or counselor.

If you have proven ability and interest in some subjects such as those I have mentioned, ask the admissions office—usually through your interviewer—if this should be brought to the attention of a department chairperson. He or she may ask to see your work or to meet with you to discuss your interest at some length.

Writing is a skill necessary for success in college, and acceptances are often encouraged by the submission of good creative, expository, or research papers. If you declare an interest in writing poetry or short stories, it makes sense to submit samples of your work. Where you can document and substantiate your interests with actual achievement, do so.

Athletic Ability

If you are an outstanding athlete in one or more sports, you should discuss the advisability of contacting the coach of that sport at your college choices with your high school coach and college counselor. Coaches who want to attract star athletes will bring these applicants to the attention of admissions committees.

However, coaches must follow recruitment regulations of the National Collegiate Athletic Association and the Association of Intercollegiate Athletics for Women. Colleges in the Ivy League also follow the Ivy League Code.

College coaches can attend high school sporting events but they are forbidden to talk directly with an athlete or his or her family or recruit on the high school campus. All discussions must be conducted on the college campus; and, at the Ivies, only after the admissions office has sent application materials to a candidate.

Often high school coaches are routinely contacted by mail. After discussion with the high school counselor, the coach may send back a list of names of qualified athletes. These students are then contacted directly by college coaches.

Coaches willing to sponsor you usually feel that they can do so only at one college, two colleges at most. If you are accepted by a college and then turn them down, the coach's reputation suffers, for he has vouched for your interest. You must be straightforward. Don't solicit special help and then reject a college's acceptance. Asking for people's support often involves a gentleman's agreement that this is the college you want most. Be sure to discuss with your high school coach how he or she feels about this.

Remember, a college coach does not make the decision to admit or deny you. Coaches' requests will be taken seriously at some colleges. Remember to coordinate your work with high school and college coaches with your work with high school and college counselors.

Campus Visits

THE campus visit should be an important part of the application process. Not every college requires or recommends an interview, but you really ought not to accept any college that you have not seen. Viewbooks, videos, and viewpoints of others should form only part of your impression of the college you will attend.

Some colleges that interest you may be far away and expensive to reach. If you feel that you want to apply based on what you have read and heard, and then see if you are accepted before you decide to visit, that can work. You will have until May 1 to let a college know your decision and can visit one or two between the time you are notified and that date.

You should visit colleges some time between the spring of your junior year and January of your senior year. Most colleges become preoccupied with putting together their freshman class between January and May.

College visits can be difficult to work into a family's busy schedule and the student's school schedule except in the summertime. Visiting colleges can be an ideal way to combine business with the pleasures of a family vacation and can take place over the summer, any other school vacation period, or over a long weekend. It is worthwhile for parents to be involved in the initial visit to a college campus. It enables parents to lend intelligent informed support and advice throughout the year of decision-making.

Summer provides an opportunity to visit colleges on a more relaxed and leisurely basis than is possible during the school year. You can spend time looking around without missing school and having to cram to catch up when you return. Faculty also become annoyed if you miss too many classes to visit colleges. Since few parents can afford time away from work, summer vacations provide a time for families to shop around together.

An *ideal* time to see campuses in action is late August or early September, before many high schools reopen. Check the college calendar, usually printed in the catalogue, to see when freshmen arrive on campus for orientation. During midsummer few if any regularly enrolled students will be on campus unless a college is on a quarter system. Teachers are likely to be away as well. Consequently, the atmosphere is different. It may even be affected by a summer-school student body that is not at all representative of the regular student population. However, the advantages of travel to colleges over the summer often outweigh the drawbacks.

Any visit is better than none, and you simply will not be able to visit as many colleges as you would like during the school year. This is especially true when the college is some distance away from your home.

Most college applicants book appointments for the fall of senior year, especially on Saturday mornings. Admissions counselors are more heavily booked in the fall and are not likely to have as much time to give you as in the summer.

By combining several colleges on a week's itinerary, you can see and compare a range of colleges—from highly selective to less selective, coed and single-sex, urban or rural—while using time efficiently.

A visit will give you a chance to see the campus—its architecture, the library, the dorms, the sports facilities, the eating hall—and the immediate area around the college. You should sign up for a guided tour so that you can see inside dorms and labs, but an interview is not necessary unless you are seriously interested and likely to apply. If a college is not far away, you may want to begin with a tour and then schedule an interview and stay overnight on a return visit, so that you also get a sense of social life and the classroom.

Use maps to plan an itinerary and compute how many miles you can realistically cover in the time you have. If you are a member of the American Automobile Association, use their travel guides. They are excellent sources of routes, restaurants, and approved motels and hotels, and list historic sites near the colleges you visit.

When you call an admissions office for an appointment, the secretary can also provide information about nearby motels and recommended routes. Several colleges have opened their dormitories to families during the summer, and it is a great way to sample dorm rooms.

Campuses are often ideal places for a picnic. Shopping for food in local markets will give you a sense of what it might feel like to live in the area, and it saves money.

Campus visits can be quite expensive if you have to factor in airfare. Hotels in urban areas are particularly costly. However, paying attention to such matters during a visit does give you and your family a realistic sense of what costs you will be taking on if you have to travel to and from a college for four years. Is the flight an easy one, or does it involve making several connections? Once you land, how difficult is it to get from the airport to the campus? These are important factors if you become a student there.

Even after a thorough exploration of colleges, students often still feel uncertain about how appropriate a particular college might be for them. We tend to want a guarantee that everything will work out well when starting up a new relationship. The truth is, there are no such guarantees about college. But a thoughtful, thorough job exploring your needs and a college's offerings and making the best match you can is the only assurance I know of that things will work out. Over 50% of American college students complete their degree at a college other than the one at which they began. Sometimes it is because the match is not right; sometimes it is because it is right up to a point and then it becomes the wiser decision to seek another school.

The best advice I can give you about choosing colleges to apply to is to trust your instincts. More important than the number of volumes in the library or the vegetarian food bar is how you felt during your visit and interview. Do not underestimate the power or importance of those feelings, beyond any prestige or peer or parental pressure you might experience to be at a certain college.

The Interview

MANY colleges, particularly small private liberal arts colleges, will require or strongly recommend that you include an on-campus interview as part of your application. Some interviews are to provide you only with information. They give you a chance to ask questions and to learn why this college and you would, or would not, be a good match. Other interviews give the admissions office a chance to evaluate you and will call for some preparation.

Experienced interviewers will engage you in conversation. A "good interview" is a dialogue that gives you an opportunity to show something of your personality and to share your ideas and concerns. In this interview you will be able to convey experiences that have mattered to you, your interests, personal qualities, achievements, and any other information about your background or academic history that will help colleges to know you better.

Some colleges conduct only group sessions, or information sessions, for you and your family to attend at scheduled times. An admissions counselor will discuss the college's admissions requirements and characteristics. You will have a chance to ask questions toward the end of such a session.

Some colleges offer interviews only with alumni in your local region. You will usually be assigned to an alumnus or alumna interviewer once you have submitted your application.

PREPARING FOR AN INTERVIEW

There are as many interview styles as there are interviewers. Yet, there are some basic tips that will help you to prepare for an effective and productive interview session.

A campus interview is generated by your call to an admissions office to set one up. You do not need to have applied to a college in order to set up an interview. In fact, an interview may be important in your decision. Telephoning for an appointment is more efficient than writing because settling on a mutually convenient time can run into lengthy correspondence. If you are planning to visit more than one college in an area, you will need a calendar in front of you to set up times that coordinate, giving yourself ample time to cover the distance between colleges and arrive on time.

Just as you want each college to show an interest in you, the college wants you to be interested in it. You do this by knowing about the college and knowing why you are looking at it. You will not want to ask if you can major in business when there is no business major. Questions about student/faculty ratio and the presence or absence of Greek life can more appropriately be answered by looking in the catalogue, viewbook, or an index. You should be able to express how you would make use of the particular college's resources and what you would contribute both in and out of the classroom.

Some points you may want to touch on are listed below:

1. Your academic accomplishments: colleges like to hear what courses you have enjoyed. Has there been one course or teacher who has opened your eyes to a new way of looking at the world or at learning?

   You might want to have with you a copy of your high school transcript. Ask your interviewer if he or she would like to see it. It will present fully the courses you have studied.

2. Special experiences that have helped to shape your outlook

and values—intellectually, socially, or personally. If you would like to explain a weak record the year your family went through relocation or a divorce, or the semester you recovered from a broken leg, the interview provides this chance.

3. Your high school. If you must impart negative impressions or information, put your responses in a positive context. Some students complain about the work load or blame a low grade on an ineffectual teacher or a personality conflict. Criticizing your school without also offering constructive suggestions for improving the system undermines your own achievements. You should show that whatever the circumstances, you have tried to come to terms with demands and limitations. Show that you have dealt with circumstances maturely.

4. Ethnic diversity, financial assistance, social life, organizations and clubs, and admissions requirements.

5. Your chances of being admitted, if you feel comfortable with your interviewer. Would the interviewer encourage you to apply? What might you do to strengthen your chances if they seem marginal? Interviewers will respond candidly, basing their reply on experience and an overview of the nature of their applicant pool.

6. A cause or a current event; some interviewers may choose to ask about this. Most will not select the topic, but rather ask you what you are interested in; if they do select the topic, do not try to fudge a response to something you know little about. Say you don't follow that topic and offer to discuss something about which you do feel knowledgeable.

7. Everyone feels complimented to be asked their advice or opinion. You may want to ask your interviewer what he or she believes to be the outstanding characteristics of the college or the students there. When they speak about their college, to parents and high school students, what do they like to talk about? Do you seem like a reasonable applicant who would fit in if you attended?

8. Consider your possible responses to such questions as:

"What is your favorite book?"
"What do you consider your greatest challenge and how did you meet it?"
"How would your best friend describe you?"
"What three adjectives would you use to describe yourself?"
"What kind of roommate would you be?"
"Why do you think we should admit you?"

9. If you are asked an off-the-wall question such as "What kind of vegetable would you be?" or "What's your epitaph?" feel free to have fun with it. There is no right or wrong answer. The interviewer might be trying to loosen you up. Do not find such questions threatening. Be just as playful and imaginative in your responses.

Most interviews will last from thirty minutes to about an hour. The length of an interview often depends on the concentration of appointments on that day; a short interview is not necessarily indicative of a poor interview. Your interviewer will signal that the interview is drawing to a close. Do not try to stretch your time or make points you think you have left out. You can always write your interviewer if you do have genuine questions later. Thank your interviewer cordially by name.

You should leave an interview with some sense of whether or not an application to that college makes sense. The interviewer cannot tell you that you will or will not be admitted, but he or she can help you to evaluate realistically the strengths or gaps in your credentials. Interviewers can also give very good opinions about the advisability of retaking SATs or the most promising topic for your personal essay.

Be sure to record at least mentally your interviewer's name with the correct spelling so that you can send a thank-you note. In this note, mention something that you liked about your talk together and the college. Personalize it. If you know that you will definitely be applying, say so.

The interviewer can become your personal contact in a process that can often make you feel like a statistic. During the year you may wish to write your interviewer a letter chronicling changes in your grades (if they are upward!), new activities, or your continued interest in the college. If a college becomes your top choice, you should tell your interviewer so.

Picturing a real person whom you have met may also help you to write essays with that personality in mind. It removes the image of your work's being read by a formidable committee of strange judges.

WHAT TO WEAR

The subject of how to dress for a college interview causes perhaps more distress between parents and children than any other single aspect of the application process.

The trick is to find a style that feels natural to you; it must, of course, be neat and clean, yet appropriate for a somewhat formal occasion. No one likes to be told what to wear, but a few general rules might help you to avoid feeling awkward and out of place wherever you go to be interviewed.

Use good sense in deciding what to wear. An alumni interview held at an executive office or Wall Street suggests a different style than an interview at an artsy college.

Jeans and sneakers are not generally appropriate for an interview. More important than the length of hair on men is whether or not it is well groomed. In a time when men as well as women wear earrings and fashionable styles, my advice to both men and women is the same: aim for good taste and simplicity. Basically, your clothes should not make a louder statement than you do. They should not capture more attention than what you have to say.

As you prepare for your college interviews, keep in mind this general advice from Leslie North, associate dean of admissions at Hamilton College:

First, find out what the interview means at each school you plan to visit. Is it purely informative, or is it evaluative? In either case, it's best to start by reading the college's brochures. The interview is an opportunity for a mutual exchange of information and gives both parties a better idea of how well they suit each other. It's best to get beyond issues of size, majors, etc., and get on to more personal subjects that can't be found in a catalogue. The interview allows the student to explain glitches in his/her record and to underline for the admissions committee particular personal strengths. Before the interview think how you'd describe your school, your family, or your community to a stranger. Be prepared to talk about your classes. Make a list of extracurricular interests and think about how you spend your time. Qualities that impress an interviewer? Honesty, openness, curiosity, independence, thoughtfulness. Remember to make eye contact with the interviewer. You'll see someone who's on your side!

After your interviews, ask yourself if you felt comfortable. Despite the anxiety you may have felt, were you able to talk openly? The admissions office is, after all, a representation of the college. It reflects the attitude of a school toward its students. Did you feel good during your visit? Trust your instincts.

COLLEGE REPRESENTATIVES

Many high schools welcome a number of college admissions representatives who visit—usually in the spring or fall—to tell you about their colleges and to meet you. These sessions are not, strictly speaking, interviews, but they will provide you with the opportunity to make a first, personal impression on a voting member of the admissions committee.

The representative who visits your school has usually established a rapport with your counselor and knows your school well. The rep will know what an A in Advanced Placement Physics at your high school represents in terms of work and achievement. Remember, working with a particular admissions person who can advocate for and interpret your candidacy to the rest of his committee during the voting sessions personalizes the application process.

Following informational sessions at your high school, the representative will often discuss candidates with the high school counselor. It is embarrassing for a counselor to mention a student who has forgotten to show up or wandered in late to the session. Take the high school visiting sessions seriously. Colleges send admissions representatives on the road at considerable expense because they think personal contact is important. So should you.

Listen to announcements and check regularly with the guidance office to see which admissions representatives are scheduled to come to your school.

To get the most from these sessions, read through catalogues and bulletins beforehand. Don't show up at the Wellesley session thinking it is Wesleyan and ask if there is a men's soccer team. If you haven't had time to read extensively, acquaint yourself with the basic facts about a college by glancing at its entry in an index.

Some colleges ask alumni to visit high schools instead of sending admissions representatives. Such alumni are acting in an official capacity. You should extend the same respect and courtesy to them that you would to a voting member of the committee. These alumni have contact with the admissions office. Many of them write a report underscoring their impressions of you. These become one more part of your application folder.

The Personal Essay

THE personal essay required by most private colleges and by some public universities is your chance to tell colleges what you would like them to know about you. It offers you an opportunity to go beyond grades and test scores and share ideas and experiences that are important to *you*.

What is the purpose of colleges' asking you to write essays? Actually, there is more than one way an essay gives colleges important insights into you.

First of all, an essay suggests how you think. A higher education will ask you to make sense of experience. To do this, you need to be able to recognize patterns of events, be able to integrate material and understand its significance, and present coherently both orally and on paper.

Secondly, along with an interview, the essay is the best means you have of conveying your interests, your ideas, your accomplishments, and your values. Colleges want to hear what has made you who you are. They want you to reflect on what has mattered to you.

Thirdly, the essay offers a chance to see what *you* think is important for colleges to know about you. After you have presented the factual information on the rest of the application, what of significance do you feel has been left unsaid?

Fourthly, the essay is a sample of your writing. It demonstrates your ability to select, organize, and present material in grammatically correct form.

Dean of Admissions at Amherst College Jane Reynolds sees the essay as "the point in the application where you have the most active voice. This voice is the most interesting part of the application process to the admissions committee."

There are several common essay topics that we shall discuss. A few rules of thumb apply, however, to just about any essay topic.

Implicit in *any* assigned topic is the question "Who are you?" A question may on the surface ask you to discuss your educational objectives, your thoughts on the importance of ethical instruction at the collegiate level, a recent invention you wish you had invented, or a person real or fictional whom you would like to invite to dinner. But whatever the topic, the motive behind the question is to get you to say something important about yourself.

What makes writing the essay such a tedious or painful exercise for so many applicants? To begin with, many topics ask you to share personal feelings and facts with strangers. Writing or talking about oneself is hard under any circumstances. How loudly should we bang our own drum? When does modesty cross the line into self-effacement?

In my experience, I have observed that most young people tell too little rather than too much about themselves.

The personal essay forces you to come to grips with some emotionally charged experiences. For instance, you may need to put a below-average academic record into context by talking about a change in family structure brought about by divorce or an extended, serious, or ultimately fatal illness of an immediate family member that was disruptive to your concentration. A complicated relationship with a friend or relative might trigger an essay about a significant lesson in the value of compromise. Some of the essays that follow demonstrate how sensitive topics, such as the serious illness of an uncle, can be written about with thoughtful objectivity.

SAMPLE QUESTIONS

There are ten basic types of essay topic that you are likely to encounter on college applications. Some examples are given from past applications. Many topics are "generic"; that is, they are used by a variety of colleges. Others are specific to individual schools.

1. THE PERSONAL EXPERIENCE ESSAY
  • Evaluate and discuss a significant experience or achievement that has special meaning to you.

2. THE ACTIVITY/INTEREST ESSAY
  • Which activity or interest has meant the most to you and why?
  • Describe an accomplishment that you have achieved with great difficulty.

3. ACADEMIC OR INTELLECTUAL EXPERIENCE
  • Describe your most significant academic experience.
  • Describe an issue of personal, local, or national concern and its importance to you.

4. A WORK OF ART
  • What is your favorite book and why?
  • Discuss the impact on you of a book, play, work of art, musical composition, or film.

5. PHILOSOPHICAL TOPICS
  • Should the study of "ethics" be a required part of every student's undergraduate curriculum? Why or why not?
    (The University of Pennsylvania)
  • "Today, young men and women no longer have heroes outside the home. Individuals who might have served as possible role models have been discovered to be too weak to emulate." Do you agree or disagree with this statement? Why?
    (Duke University)

6. PEOPLE
  • If you could interview a prominent person (past or present), whom would you choose and why?

- Discuss your idea of an honorable person.
- Choose a person who has had a significant influence on you, and describe that influence.

7. DIVERSITY
- Diversity among people continues to be a unique blend of cultures and enriches the university community. Briefly describe the environment in which you grew up and how it has influenced your interests, your values, and your thinking about sexism, racism, and prejudice.

(Tufts University)
- Describe an experience that has resulted in your knowledge of a culture other than your own.

8. THE CREATIVE ESSAY
- You have been appointed editor of a major news publication. Write your first editorial for the year 2000.
- Describe your life at age forty. What have you chosen to do and why? What are you proudest of?
- Write your own recommendation, evaluating your strengths and weaknesses.
- You have answered many questions on the application, all asked by someone else. If you were in a position to ask a provocative and revealing question of college applicants, what would that question be? Now that you have asked your ideal question, answer it.   (Dartmouth College)
- You have been elected to speak at your high school or college graduation. What will you say? Write your speech.   (Goucher College)

9. WORK SAMPLES
Increasingly, small liberal arts colleges ask applicants to submit an essay done for a class with the teacher's comments and a grade.

The purpose is twofold: the writing sample represents

what you regard as your best work; and it cannot be adjusted to suit a college application. It has already been submitted for evaluation and that evaluation stands. It is important to include a brief explanation of the assignment.

Whether or not a request for a graded paper is part of an application, I urge you to submit it. Do not hesitate to ask the advice of a teacher on choosing the most representative of your most insightful and well-presented work.

10. EXPLAIN YOUR CHOICE TO APPLY

- Describe why you have chosen this university as the place to pursue your educational and/or career goals.
- We know that you are not just like any other applicant, and we have a firm conviction that we are not just like any other college. Why do you think the College of the University of Chicago might be a good place for you to be a student?
- What are you hoping will be the outcome of your college education?   (The University of Denver)

It is important to make your response as specific as possible. Spend time looking at the way the college presents itself in its viewbook. Show that you have taken the time to learn what the college values about its educational resources or style. Then discuss your personal and educational objectives and needs and explain how you think you can meet them there. It is equally as important to say what you will contribute to classroom and community as to say what resources you will use.

TIPS ON ESSAY WRITING

Before we look at some samples of student essays, there are some tips to keep in mind:

1. An effective essay begins with self-evaluation. Think over the possible responses. Which will tell the most about you?
2. Don't think your experience has to be exotic, rare, or bizarre. There is a genuine appeal to an event we can all relate to. It is interesting to learn what you see as significant in ordinary occurrences—an observation, a change, a chance encounter.
3. After you have selected an experience, person, idea, or event about which to write, find a focus, a pattern, a common thread that unifies the experience and the essay. You don't want your essay to be nothing more than a list of activities or observations. What differentiates an essay from a list are connections you make and significances you find and discover about what has happened to you. An essay discusses what experience has meant to you, how it has shaped your development, your thinking, your way of seeing, and your values.
4. Ask if your essay or statement matters. Would you want to meet the person who wrote it? Is it enjoyable and interesting to read? Remember, your essay might be the fortieth or the hundredth an admissions counselor is reading at 1 A.M. the morning before April 14! Does it hold the reader's attention? Even at 1 A.M.?
5. Is there a voice behind the essay? Is a real person talking, or is the language artificial, stiff, and inflated?

Too often students write what they think colleges want to hear, rather than what they would like to say. I am not at all convinced such a formula exists: colleges want to hear only the essay that you believe it is important to write.

Sometimes it helps to write your essay with a person in mind. Maybe you have met someone at a college fair or at your high school from the college. Write your essay imagining that real person reading it. Don't forget that flesh and blood people do read these essays.

Often when students feel blocked, I recommend that they

talk their experiences into a cassette recorder. Play it back
and listen to your voice. This technique can help you to
overcome a too-formal, stilted style. Speak as though you are
sharing your experience with a friend. If you write as though
you are sharing rather than lecturing or preaching, your
essay will have a natural style.

6. Have confidence in what you write. You should feel willing
   to stand behind every statement.
7. Keep your writing and diction simple. Very few students can
   write jokey or gimmicky essays that work.

   Students often say to me that they wish they could write a
   creative essay. They equate "creative" with adventurous
   forms and brilliantly witty prose. Creative college essays are,
   in fact, those that are real and reflect you. If you are adventurous or brilliantly witty, then perhaps your essay will be
   too. But if you share your own particular experience, because you are unique your essay will be "creative."
8. Approach your essay with honesty. Students wonder if some
   subjects are taboo. No subject in itself is right or wrong,
   good or bad. It is what you make of your subject that counts.
   I have read stunning essays about a meeting between two
   dissimilar people who became friends or a difficult encounter with an old friend. It *is* important, however, to avoid
   clichés or neatly packaged "happy endings" or the "now I am
   all grown up because I have known suffering" approach.

With any topic such as a difficult learning experience or a
challenge of a divorce in the family or an illness, it is important
that you are clear enough about how you have emerged more self-
aware or compassionate before you write. A certain objectivity
shows that you have reflected upon the experience and worked hard
to understand it, how it has changed you, and why that change is
important. If you still feel bitter about your parents' divorce or your
suspension from school in eleventh grade for rude behavior toward
a classmate, then you are probably not ready to write about it for a

college essay. You must have your conflict resolved in order to write about such a subject. You should be able to describe that conflict with fairness and openness, if you choose to write about it at all.

SAMPLE STUDENT ESSAYS

In the essay below, this student uses two contrasting episodes— work on a corn and soybean farm in Iowa and an annual visit to the Chicago Board of Trade to follow the prices of soybeans—to show how they have broadened his knowledge and his experience. Notice how the writer uses a symbol, a handkerchief, in each section as a way of joining the two episodes. This is a good example of a response to an essay topic that asks you to write about a meaningful personal experience.

"Hey, Tim! Watch it out there! You knocked out two rows of corn the last time through." Tim nodded and waved his hand in assent as the tractor he was driving turned and plowed down the next row dragging the burrowing cultivator behind it. The hot sun immediately started baking the fresh turned soil behind Tim. I wiped my brow with an old red handkerchief as I got back into the truck to go over to the other field. The days are long patrolling the cornfields of Iowa during the summer, but I have learned to appreciate the responsibility of my summer job. For the past three summers, I have been employed by my father as a manager of two of our farms north of Ottumwa, Iowa. My tasks range from hiring and supervising workers to operating a tractor to fixing fences.

"Sell short at three-two-four. Go with it. Ride that trend." The barking voices of the soybean traders grew louder as the menacing hands of the clock neared one o'clock. The huge electronic scoreboard instantaneously flashed the fluctuating prices of soybeans as crowds of mesmerized onlookers watched. I wiped the perspiration from my forehead with my freshly laundered handkerchief. Over the years, making a trip to the Chicago Board of Trade has become an annual event for my father and me. Our knowledge of the conditions of the

crops back in Iowa has proved to be a valuable asset in speculating on the price of commodity futures. Researching weather patterns and crop conditions is a very important job for me. By forecasting the drought of 1988, we were able to hedge our crop by selling corn and soybeans commodities before the price dropped lower.

These two experiences, although very different in their atmosphere, are similar in that they have given me the opportunity to take on large responsibilities. Working on the farm has provided me with leadership experience and improved my communication skills. My research work for the monetary aspect of our farm operation has allowed me to learn the financial side of a business operation. My jobs not only brought me earnings but also knowledge and experience.

The following essay was written in response to the topic "Discuss a person who has had an influence on you." This writer selected her favorite uncle, but she avoids sentimentality by going beneath the surface of her uncle's illness to examine her own reaction to it.

I did my best. I sat by the bedside, giggling and telling jokes and making small talk as I always did. But this time, I realized that my stories were really awfully dumb and that I was laughing much too loudly. I sounded like a TV laugh track that reminds everybody to laugh when something is supposed to be funny. That wasn't what I wanted to be doing at all—smiling and laughing and talking about school. Uncle Martin was very sick. He knew it, and I knew it. I tried to pretend everything was well, but pretending was all it was, and I couldn't do that to my favorite uncle.

Magazines cover the countertops, and books are crowded in the cases. My uncle's house holds more information inside it than a library. It is my sanctuary. I realize now that from the things we shared—all the learning and talking and listening and reading—I have learned to love the quest for knowledge. We've discussed and debated so much, be it current events or things that happen in school. My uncle has always treated me as an intelligent, thinking person. That is probably one of the reasons that I've always respected him so. And it is because of his encouragement that I can believe that I am bright and that I am capable.

It is very bizarre. My uncle has been bound to a wheelchair for all my life, and for most of his own. And I never believed that there was anything wrong with him. Uncle Martin explained polio to me when I was very young. I don't recall his exact words, but I do remember that my heart could not understand how he could be so cool, so nonchalant about this "bad" disease that had robbed him of his youth.

I realized much later that Uncle Martin had not lied to me. He was quite comfortable with his sickness. I was the one who needed help. I was the one who was making everything awkward. And I think that it had been my instinct to want to get angry, and want to blame his pain on something or somebody. When I saw his peace, it made me uncomfortable. Now I see Uncle Martin's situation as a much bigger, more encompassing, one. No matter which direction his disease drags him, towards health or sickness, the importance is on how we deal with it, what it means to us, what it has taught us. I have learned from Uncle Martin in the hospital bed that it is pointless to fight some things, and useless to argue about things like "fair" and "unfair." Because after you walk away for a while—leave the hospital room, or close your bedroom door—you see a bigger picture and a larger reality. Uncle Martin will be fine, not because his doctors say so and not because they're moving him out of I.C.U. and he might come home next week. He'll be fine because he understands the meaning of this; he does not need to run away from it, as I felt I did. The happiness and satisfaction that he drew from his life— from the time we spent together, learning and sharing and talking— will comfort and guide him and take care of him. I do not have to take care of him. I must just keep visiting, and caring, and loving him. No problem—he's my favorite uncle.

In the next essay, the writer sees in a trip to a foreign place the inner journey she has experienced. The essay turns on the relationship formed between her and a native child to show the importance of making meaningful connections.

Sitting on the plane, I picture myself being greeted at the Airport by my parents. I arrive clad in African garb, gift-laden, and holding five-year-old Mikey. This image is only a fantasy, but such an affinity for children is not out of character for me.

Everything in my past experience with children should have prepared me for the attachment I developed for Mikey. However, it took even me by surprise and affected me deeply. I had gone to Kenya with a group of twelve students and two leaders through an organization that operates international cross-cultural programs. My initial reasons for going to Africa were to photograph the people and animals of Kenya and to participate in a community service project in a small Kenyan village. However, I was immediately attracted to the seven native children in the family with whom I lived. Returning home each afternoon from the service project, I would be greeted on the road leading to our house by seven smiling faces. The children would excitedly offer to carry any books, tools, or packages I was holding. Their desire to please me and have me share in their fun continued into the evening activities when they would sing, dance, and recite prayers and poems. As much as I enjoyed these group rituals, I found myself spending more time with Mikey than with the other children.

Mikey was especially outgoing, inquisitive, and enthusiastic to be the subject of my photographs. Though I spoke little Swahili, and he spoke even less English, communication was not a problem. He was as eager to learn from me as I was to learn from him. I taught him the rhyme of "The Itsy Bitsy Spider" and how to make paper airplanes, and he taught me his version of exotic dances. Within just a few days, we had begun developing a strong relationship. Mikey's attempt to learn the alphabet is a memorable example of his adventuresome personality. The first time I sang the alphabet, Mikey was immediately fascinated by it. He eagerly tried to copy the words and rhyme, but had awkward, disappointing results. He laughed off his mistakes, determined to master the task. Eventually, he was successful because he never stopped trying.

When I returned home from a two-day trip away from the village, Mikey's mother explained to me that he repeatedly asked for "teacher" while I was gone. Realizing his eagerness to learn and my

*capacity to influence him, I began spending more time with him,
further strengthening our friendship.*

*As long as I can remember, I have always had a strong feeling for
younger children. At first I merely liked to play with them. When I
became interested in photography in grade school, I liked to photograph other children. During my past three years in high school I
have been exposed to opportunities to become more actively involved
with children. My first involvement began when I became a member
of the Save The Children chapter in my school. In eleventh grade I
was appointed President, giving me a chance to help more personally
the four children we sponsor world wide. This involvement with Save
The Children is what encouraged me to go to the African village and
build a community poultry farm. The summer between tenth and
eleventh grades I worked as an art counselor at a day camp. Having
always enjoyed art, I relished the opportunity to teach four to twelve-
year-olds. Last year, I volunteered to be in an organization called
Kids Helping Kids that has high school students meet with groups of
seventh and eighth graders, the purpose being to present younger
students with a person they can talk to who is between a peer and a
parent. Individually, each of these activities has a different purpose
and meaning to me, yet collectively they represent and exemplify
what I do most naturally and enjoy most.*

*For two weeks Mikey allowed me to be his "teacher," friend, and
photographer, encompassing all these activities and inspiring me to
pursue my enjoyment and interest in working with children. It was
not the fact that Mikey was of a culture different from mine that
made my relationship with him so special. It was that Mikey represented the qualities in children I admire, respect, and try to preserve
in myself. Being uninhibited, he was willing to take risks. He was
affectionate and accepting. His feelings were genuine and his personality unaffected. In identifying these qualities in children, I have
developed a greater sense of my own identity and values. The importance of connections between people lies in the power of individual
growth.*

The young woman who wrote the essay below discusses the
importance of sports in her life. She uses two sports—one a team

sport and one an individual sport—to contrast their demands and challenges. It is also an example of a strong feminist stand that is not strident or bitter. She has really stepped back from the prejudice she has experienced and worked to understand her response to it.

Sports have always been important to me. They have not only been fun, but they have also taught me about many of life's basic principles. Through sports I have experienced the agony of defeat and the thrill of victory. The challenge of sports has helped me to develop into a strong, independent person. The two sports that have been most meaningful to me are tennis and ice hockey. Playing on the boys' hockey team for three years and on an all girls' club hockey team for four years has taught me the value of team work in the pursuit of common goals. One person cannot support the team alone. Everyone needs to do his or her part and work together as a solid unit. A team cannot win without its members interacting selflessly and with camaraderie and support.

Playing on the boys' hockey team has been a particularly valuable experience because it has made me a stronger person willing to stand up for what I believe in. I was doing something different from the norm, and some people disapproved. These people held the misconception that I had joined the team to prove that I was as good as the boys, presumably driven by misguided women's liberation motives. This was not my intention at all. I initially joined the team because I love the sport, and since there was no existing girls' team, playing with the boys was the next best thing. Although my team was supportive, I encountered some prejudiced and surprised parents, opponents, and spectators. On the way to the girls' locker room, I often overheard parents and players whispering, "Oh, this game is going to be a cinch. They have a girl on the team." Whenever I heard something like that, it made me try twice as hard. It soon became important to me to prove that a girl can be competitive on a boys' team. I have always given 100% on the ice not only because I love the sport, but also because I want to be the very best at whatever I do. I knew that if I ever got hurt during a game or made a poor play, people would say, "Well, she shouldn't have been out there in the was excitement, warmth and laughter, and again the group looked to their song leader with respect and admiration. Only this time, that song leader was I.

During the course of my junior year, I had spent countless frustrating hours straining my fingers into contorted positions learning new chords, developing new and awkward rhythms, and practicing until my guitar strings drew blood. Despite the threats of friends to set my instrument in flames because of the awful sound it produced in those trying first months, I remained determined in my struggle. Oddly, however, the more I improved, the less I found it necessary to perform and impress others. Playing the guitar became something I savor for myself. Today, I continue to teach myself the guitar, but now it is principally a source of relaxation and an important measure of personal accomplishment for me.

The ability to educate myself has served me well in my scholastic pursuits, especially in a large public school. The sheer number of students and the size of teachers' workloads make it difficult for even the most attentive teacher to offer much time outside the classroom. Unstructured discussion time or meetings which allow ideas to germinate, new projects to take shape or old truths to be discovered are a luxury simply not available. I thus had to take the initiative and seek assistance on a personal level or make use of the available resources, both in and out of school, to find the answers on my own.

I was very fortunate to have spent my grade school years in a small, nurturing private school. There, I was encouraged to pursue my intellectual curiosity, and my thoughts and ideas found respect and support. The self-confidence and love of learning fostered in those early years have served me well, not only in an academic setting, but in my endeavors, such as teaching myself to play the guitar.

College and graduate school will again afford me a few more years to luxuriate in a total education experience, confronting issues, discovering answers, and pondering ideas without the intrusion of an often conflicting reality. While I look forward to that privilege, at some point, formal education ends, leaving three-quarters of one's life yet ahead. The task of educating oneself, of finding solutions to new and greater challenges, must continue with one's every breath.

first place," or, "It was bound to happen sooner or later." I refused to allow that kind of talk to be proven.

Tennis, in contrast to ice hockey, is an individual sport. It demands intense concentration, self-discipline, and positive thinking. The mental toughness and perseverance I learned on the tennis court have helped me significantly in my academic life. It takes the same kind of discipline to practice math problem after math problem as it does to hit forehand after forehand. The power of positive thinking that tennis requires has also affected other areas of my life. During every match I continually tell myself, "Come on, you can do it. Hang in there." I often use these same thoughts, for example, to spur me on to a successful completion of a difficult paper topic or test.

Throughout my four years of varsity tennis, I have been a doubles player. Tennis doubles adds a different dimension to the game of tennis than singles. Dealing with three other people on the court introduces many more variables into a match than are involved in singles tennis. Strategies are more complex, and therefore intellect becomes more important. Doubles has also taught me how to deal with people in a one on one situation. Having a supportive relationship with my partner is paramount for success. One has to learn to help each other out when the going gets tough. As a result of my doubles team experience, I have become more sensitive to other people's needs and emotions.

In the following sample, the student uses the personal essay to discuss an unpleasant episode that occurred at boarding school to explain his sudden change of school and, more importantly, to show how his lapse in judgment taught him something important. The writer successfully achieves an objective point of view about an incident of dishonesty and discusses how he was forced by it to grow up.

My wrongdoing had begun with thrillseeking. My boarding school roommate and I, along with a few friends, used to sneak out of our rooms at night and find ways to get into buildings and streak by the security guards, hoping they'd chase us. However, just as a drug addict needs more and more to get high, these thrills soon were not enough and could not slake my thirst for adventure. So I began using another student's credit card, not out of malice for anyone, but really for thrills. I wasn't breaking into anything or physically removing objects, so it never felt as though I had stolen anything. It was only the reactions of several of my fellow students that made me begin to see that I had done wrong, very wrong.

It was only upon returning to the dorm that I began to look upon myself as something other than a harmless joker. When several of our friends came in and began to talk with us, I started to feel embarrassed. I suddenly realized that I was worse than those who drank or took drugs: I had stolen from a friend and had violated the trust that fellow students place in one another in dormitory situations to respect each other's privacy. When I realized that I was now "famous" on campus, I became even more embarrassed and hid in my room, ashamed of myself for causing all my friends to distrust me.

My embarrassment and shame was heightened when I had to call my parents and tell them to pick me up because I had been expelled. Instead of the hysterical reaction I had anticipated, they were caring and tried to understand. I realized that instead of being angry, they and everybody else were disappointed in me. I had finally straightened out my grades and sports and was performing up to everybody's expectations that year, but now I had shot myself in the foot. I too became disappointed in myself, but, instead of drowning in a sea of self-pity, I resolved to funnel my disappointment in a positive direction.

My family and I began seeing a family therapist and I a psychologist on my own. Whereas I had been reclusive and secretive about my life, I became more open with my parents. I found it easier to communicate my feelings to them instead of bottling them up inside. This openness continued into my new school when I found an easier time making friends and therefore wasn't as reclusive and emotionally detached as I had been. I also found I began studying harder, and instead of other people expecting me to perform academically, I expected it of myself. I began to take pride in my school spirit, a feeling which at boarding school I had chosen to ignore. I also was forced to grow up emotionally and take charge of my life as I left the security blanket that boarding school provided its students

through forced study periods and a structured existence. I now regulated my own hours. I would no longer have a full-time faculty to push me forward. I would have to push myself. I feel that I have responded to this onus. My study habits are more consistent and I make sure my work is done to my satisfaction instead of quickly doing an assignment and then going out. Since my expulsion from boarding school, my road has been rocky but I feel that the whole experience, in terms of growing up and taking responsibility for my life, may have helped me far more than another year at boarding school ever could have.

In response to the request "Tell us something about yourself that we have not learned anywhere else in the application," the student below uses a skill he has developed on his own to talk about his tendency to pursue interests independently, a quality useful in college.

It started on one of my first evenings at camp during a "song session" when a few hundred of us packed the dining room. Suddenly, a man emerged with a guitar and, standing in front of the fireplace, began to play. The reaction of my peers was phenomenal. Friends and strangers joined hands, clapped, swayed, and cheered. I can still envision a small deaf child, who surely felt excluded from many other group activities, singing along by reading the words and feeling the vibrations of the music through a table. I felt a sense of excitement and warmth during that song session that I will never forget. I sensed the respect and admiration of my peers for our song leader, I saw the reaction of the girls to a "musician," and I envisioned myself in that same role. And so, the very next day, I borrowe[d] a friend's guitar and began to teach myself to play.

A year later, I was spending the summer in Israel on an arch[ae]ological dig. One evening, still invigorated from the excitemen[t] uncovering with my own hands a 3,000 year old olive press c[ut] into bedrock from the King Solomon era, I found myself sitting my friends on the beaches of Caesarea looking out over a Med[iterra]nean sunset beneath the shadow of an ancient Roman am[phithe]ater. Again there was a campfire, again there was music, aga[in]

Hopefully, I will have learned to pick up a challenge or a goal, as I picked up the guitar, and pursue it successfully.

The final example represents a creative approach to a question that asks: "Which invention has had the greatest impact on life in the twentieth century?" The writer has chosen to reveal an interest of importance to him—skiing—and a sense of humor. Instead of citing the atomic bomb or penicillin, he chooses to write about the artificial snowmaker. Without being flippant, he answers the question with originality. This approach is creative, yet the essay is clear, substantive, straightforward, and self-revealing.

There's nothing quite like the feeling of getting off a chairlift and slowly sliding to the top of a particular trail. As you stand there, high above the distant village below, a certain sense of power grabs hold of your arms and legs. Filling your lungs with cold mountain air gives you the confidence to snap your skis downhill and plunge down the face of the steep, narrow path which represents your enemy. The wind pounds into your face as you cut and slash curves into the soft, white trail. Your mind battles with itself as your instincts for speed seek to overrule your conscience for safety. In a few quick minutes the battle is over and you arrive at the base of the mountain. You are both exhausted and exhilarated, and eager to do it again.

Skiing has become somewhat of an obsession with me. The problem is that the big and challenging (interesting) mountains are usually too far away, and the ones nearby seem to never have enough snow for worthwhile skiing. Lately, a new hope has arisen for us dedicated "slopesters." The artificial snowmaker has burst onto the scene to revitalize skiing in the northeast. These machines allow ski areas to maintain favorable conditions when there isn't enough natural snowfall. Snowmakers are so popular and practical that almost every ski area utilizes them to please their customers. With larger quantities of snow, skiing is more enjoyable and the season lasts further into the spring. For me this has also meant more hours of death-defying speeds and high-velocity crashes than would have been possible otherwise.

The machine, itself, is actually quite interesting. At subfreezing temperatures, water and air are pumped through two giant hoses into a contraption that resembles an airplane engine. The two substances are then combined and thrust outward by a gigantic fan. These noisy beasts of science then scatter their precious snow across acres of steep, rocky terrain for countless maniacs to enjoy despite the frigid temperatures.

I'm sure that whoever invented the artificial snowmaker grins with delight whenever he thinks of the problems faced by people who try to ski through the dispersing snow. The deafening roar and blinding whiteness of the "mini-blizzard" are enough to bring skiers to their knees. It's often hard enough to navigate the trees, chairlift poles, and fellow skiers without the diversion created by the snowmakers. Introducing momentary blindness and deafness to the challenge allows for some rather scary moments and unsightly mishaps. It's safe to say, however, that I'd rather be defeated by a snowmaker's blizzard than by a rock, uncovered by lack of snow.

Although the snowmaker doesn't carry with it the international impact of the atomic bomb or the space shuttle, its effects are important to me on a more personal level. Its existence has allowed me to better enjoy the rewarding and relaxing sport of skiing. This machine gives me the chance to test myself and to find out just how far I can push my skill and courage. To me, these are the true benefits of the artificial snowmaker.

A Case in Point: One Student's Successful Approach

I AM not a great believer in the case-study approach to understanding college admissions. While it is useful to know median test scores for admitted students and to have a sense of who has been admitted from your high school in recent years to the various colleges, such data should serve only as a reasonable guide, not as a prescription. Each individual has strong points and limitations for any college. Each is unique.

I offer the following case of James only as an example of a highly qualified student's making a right match for himself. That should, after all, be the goal of each of you in the college application process.

A student at a college-preparatory public high school, James had scores, grades, and personal accomplishments that gave him a good shot at several highly selective colleges. His strengths were a rigorous course selection: five years of Latin, three of Greek, and three of French. The summer after his junior year James had also acquired a working knowledge of sign language while employed as a counselor at a camp with many deaf students. In effect, James was familiar with five languages, including English. That he had taken it upon himself to acquire sign language was a mark of his ingenuity and willingness to attempt new things. Four years of science, including senior chemistry at the Advanced Placement level, four years of math, culminating in calculus AB, and three years of theater for arts credit in addition to English and history produced a transcript that showed follow-through, continuity, and challenge. From ninth grade to twelfth, James went from a B+ average to an A− in tenth grade to an A in eleventh and twelfth grades. This achievement placed James about twelfth in his class of 150. And every year James took at least one course beyond the required five.

Standardized testing was high in math and excellent in verbal, 730 and 660, respectively. The Achievement Test average was 650. Of some concern to highly selective colleges would be his English Composition Achievement score of 580. A TSWE of 53 indicated that for much improvement to take place, James would need to commit to considerable time for review of English grammar and usage. He was a good writer who earned B+'s in English courses. In conference with his counselor, the decision was reached to leave the English Achievement as it was and to convince colleges that he could, after all, write, by submitting strong essays and a recommendation from an English teacher. James also included a writing sample of a paper done for American history in eleventh grade with teacher comments and a grade.

After a summer that included ten college campus visits, James knew by early October that his two top choices were an Ivy League university and a small, highly selective liberal arts college with a Friends tradition. James's credentials qualified him for both, but now he needed to look at what he had to offer beyond statistics to see how he might target his applications with focus and a keen sense of a match between himself and one college.

James had devoted his time outside class to a church youth group of which he was president, to tutoring at a neighborhood community organization, and to counseling at a summer camp for children with disabilities. He was someone who acted on his beliefs about the need to reach out to others by becoming directly and significantly involved.

James checked the median SAT scores listed by each of his choices. For the Ivy he was 30 points below the verbal median and 40 points above the math. For the liberal arts college, he was only 10 points below the verbal median and 20 points above on the math. His English Achievement score was 60 points below the median for each.

James also learned that three other very strong applicants from his class had chosen to apply Early Decision to the Ivy. He learned from his high school counselor that he was below them in scores and in class rank. James knew how to interact effectively with his counselor, and their discussions yielded important information, so that James could make an informed decision.

During his interview at the small college James had felt that the veteran interviewer was interested in his work on behalf of others. Because James had discussed his interests carefully beforehand with his counselor, he went into his interview able to talk about his interest in language and communication—everything from classical languages to modern to sign language. Even his interest in the theater and in teaching were related to his overall larger interest in communication. James saw a theme in his interests. The interviewer really picked up on that theme, partly because of the college's firm commitment to community. The Quaker tradition puts a strong emphasis on self-governance, concern for others, and personal as well as intellectual growth.

James's Ivy interview had been scheduled to take place with an alumnus only after he had submitted his application, and he felt that that decision on the part of the college told him something important about the difference between a large and a small, more personalized college. James felt he would not have quite the same chance at the Ivy to establish a connection with a member of the admissions committee and that that fact reflected an important tone of the college.

When James announced to his counselor his plan to apply Early Decision to the small liberal arts college, the counselor was delighted by the rightness of the match. The reaction of many of James's peers was, however, quite different. Some of his friends felt that he was settling for less prestige by not holding out for the Ivy, even though the small college had a superb reputation. He encountered peer pressure at its most snobbish and uninformed worst.

James had done his research. He had consulted with his counselor. He knew where he was most likely to be admitted Early. He liked both colleges equally well. The strength of James's application was how well he knew himself. As a student he knew he could elect a strong curriculum and do exceptionally well. As a community member, he chose his interests carefully, limited himself to these interests over the years, and attained leadership positions. James had been his own person. He trusted his instincts about how comfortable he felt on the campus of the small liberal arts college and remembered how important relationships were to him, such as the one he enjoyed with the interviewer.

James was admitted Early Decision, while two of the three more statistically qualified applicants to the Ivy were deferred, and only the top-ranked candidate was admitted.

The moral of James's story is that you need to assess realistically where your particular credentials and accomplishments are most likely to be well-received and valued. Different colleges, as we have discussed, put different emphasis on each aspect of the application. And the competition from within your own school is definitely a factor, although it need not wholly determine your choices. James used information available to him effectively. He also trusted his instincts.

James did what effective counseling should help you to do—he made a good match. He did not go only for an Ivy label, nor did he allow peer pressure to influence him. This principle remains true at any level of competitiveness. Choose a college that values you and your achievements. It is the best start for a successful and happy four years of college.

The Colleges Respond

I F you apply Early Decision or Early Action, you will receive a letter of acceptance, deferment, or denial in December. Under regular admission, you will receive the results in mid-April. There is little you can do between the time you submit your applications and have your interviews and the time you hear from the colleges. Just keep working and inform the colleges of your progress and school involvement, as I have discussed.

If you are accepted by more than one college, you may wish to revisit the schools, sit in on classes, and look around again before deciding among them. Never accept any college sight unseen. Be sure to withdraw formally—by letter—from those colleges you decide not to attend. You should do this by their reply deadline so that the colleges can inform students on the Wait List of openings.

A letter of deferment or of Wait List status calls for you to put more effort into promoting your candidacy.

Deferred Early Decision applicants should sit down with their counselor and review their applications. Try to assess your chances of a regular acceptance realistically. Counselors can often learn if something specific precluded an acceptance. In a couple of months until regular decisions are made, you can work to strengthen your candidacy. Consider the following:

1. Were letters of support effective and strong? If not, can someone else support your candidacy?

2. Will you be involved in special projects or activities through-out the year? Should you bring these to the attention of the admissions committee?
3. Should you submit any recent work samples that have earned praise?
4. Have you been elected to any positions of leadership in school or community groups since you last applied? Have you been awarded any honors or team letters?
5. Was your interview not a success? Some colleges will grant you a second or an alumni interview upon request.
6. Should you consider writing to the college and stating *specifically* why you think that college is right for you and what you think you can offer to this *particular* college community?

If you find yourself in the precarious Wait List category, what should you do?

The Wait List is reserved for those applicants who will be granted admission only if admitted members choose not to enroll, thereby opening up more spaces. Sometimes sufficient spaces will not open up until as late as August. Meanwhile, you will have to place a nonrefundable deposit at a second-choice college where you have been accepted, in order to secure a place there.

Some colleges rank their candidates on the Wait List. Seek your counselor's help to discover where you stand. In any one year, colleges can usually predict how many students they will invite off the Wait List and tell you whether or not you should feel hopeful.

Note, too, that in the Wait List situation, substantial financial aid need may hinder your chances; by this time, most scholarship money has been appropriated.

If you don't mind the prolonged anxiety of the Wait List, then stick with it. However, there are some things you should do in the interim.

Declaring your interest is the best way to improve your chances of gaining entry.

Colleges will send a card to you and ask that you return it, telling them whether or not you wish to remain on their Wait List. This alone will not sufficiently improve your chances.

You can show your interest by writing a letter to the director of admissions. Say why you want to go there and that you definitely will attend if given the chance.

If any work has earned you special praise since submitting your application, send it along.

Ask your counselor if there is anything noteworthy to mention about your grades at this time.

Although some colleges discourage another personal visit, others welcome one. If granted a second visit, try to meet a second member of the admissions team and add his support to your candidacy.

Above all, be tactful, not pushy. Some families panic and pull out what they think are the "big guns"—recommendations from senators, important or generous alumni, and trustees. *Be careful.* In most cases, admissions are best left to the professional judgment of admissions personnel.

The Applicant with a Learning Disability

IF you are reading this section, you are most probably a student with a complicated learning history, the parent of a student who has a learning disability, or a counselor advising both student and parent.

The nature of learning disabilities is difficult to comprehend, partly because they take so many different forms. Learning disabilities manifest themselves as low concentration and poor study habits, a negative attitude toward school, weak hand/eye coordination, dysgraphia, disorganization, and difficulty in sequencing verbal and mathematical symbols, among other subtle behaviors. There is much literature that discusses in depth the nature and treatment of learning disabilities.

Students with learning disabilities can and do go on to college and succeed. Their placement, however, is even more sensitive than that of students without learning disabilities. They often have low self-esteem when it comes to school. They know they are bright and capable but worry that they will be perceived as incapable. Their grades are frequently lower than their ability, and standardized testing is below average.

A student with a suspected learning disability first has to get a diagnosis. This is best done by a trained psychologist. If your school cannot provide this service, you may need to consult a psychologist privately. Your family doctor should be helpful, too, because he or she will have a medical history available. These documents will become essential to your application if you apply to a college with a learning disability support system and special admission for students with a learning disability. Documentation needs to be from testing that is not over three years old.

Standardized examinations used for college admission, such as the SAT, ACT, and Achievement Tests, can be taken on an extended time or untimed basis. An asterisk next to your score indicates that the test was given on a nonstandard basis. Arrangements for nonstandardized testing are made through your guidance counselor or college adviser. Someone from your school will be designated to administer the test to you.

In some cases, it is advisable first to take the test timed and then untimed or with extended time. If your disability is not severe, and you can perform adequately on the standard test, the two scores in combination will provide a useful measurement of what difference the extra time makes to your performance.

Directories, such as the ones by Peterson or Lovejoy in the bibliography, list those colleges that have learning support services, such as the University of Colorado, Boulder; Curry College, Milton, Massachusetts; Arizona State University, Tempe; and San Diego State University. These entries describe requirements for admission, the number of students served, available tutoring, and basic skills remediation.

I urge families to visit the learning center and speak with the director or a staff counselor. You should see the facility for yourself. Some colleges require you to take their own placement test to qualify for special admission and to have an interview with a learning resource counselor.

If it is possible financially, students who score well below expectation on standardized tests can benefit from taking a standard IQ test, such as the Wechsler Adult Intelligence Scale Revised. A low score on an SAT is often mistakenly equated with a lack of intelligence, usually by the student himself, which brings doubts about self-worth. Well administered, the WAIS-R can shed light on a student's test-taking style. It is not the score itself that is necessarily useful for college admission, but rather the diagnosis rendered by a professional administrator of the test of what the relationships among various subscores on the test reveal about the test-taker's ability to work with verbal and mathematical symbols under timed conditions. For instance, some students read well with comprehension, but it takes longer than average time.

Standardized test scores from the SAT or ACT that are unexplainably low—that is, out of sync with other measurements of aptitude and achievement—can be mystifying if submitted without any interpretation. The common cry, "My test scores just don't reflect my ability," is not sufficient in itself to be convincing. While not every college will be willing to overlook low test scores, even with explanation, you will find others appreciative of your efforts to provide documentation to explain your learning pattern.

Whatever you learn in the course of IQ testing is bound to be helpful as you continue to confront standardized testing in your college years. You may not ever become skillful at this kind of performance, but at least you can understand where it breaks down for you. Sometimes, too, knowing the facts about your learning patterns will help you to relax more about taking timed tests. That in itself can be the beginning of your doing better on them.

The Transfer Applicant

THE decision to transfer from one college to another is a difficult one because you will leave behind the familiar, just as you did only a year or so before when you left high school. You will leave behind newly formed friendships and, in some cases, course credits that cannot be transferred. Yet, slightly over half of American college students do not complete their degree at the college where they first enroll. They are willing to risk the disruption and different social and academic challenges for the promises the new college holds.

Most students who wish to transfer do so for one of two main reasons: they are unhappy and therefore unwilling to endure the academic demands of their college or they have decided on an academic concentration and believe their current college cannot meet their needs. These are the most valid and compelling reasons to transfer. If you are not feeling good about where you are, you are likely to find academic success difficult and the experience of college unpleasant. No doubt, those who keep telling you that college should be the best time of your life are setting the stage for some disillusionment; however, you should feel good about how you are growing and changing socially, personally, and academically. In the 1960s there was a stigma attached to transferring. The assumption was that those who did couldn't cut it where they were or were running away from something. That is no longer true. You should give very careful thought, however, to why and where you will transfer.

Some seniors choose the best college they are admitted to, with the idea that they will work hard, build their credentials, and apply to a more selective college after one or two years. Indeed, selective colleges will evaluate with interest your demonstrated ability to do college-level work. Most will also want to see your high school transcript, and some will even require your SAT or ACT scores. Do not approach a transfer with the idea that you will start with a completely clean slate. In general, you will need at least a 2.0 grade point average to receive consideration. Some highly selective colleges will look for a 3.0 or better.

Once in college, students do begin to clarify their goals and objectives. Impressive transfer applications are those that include an essay, whether required or not, in which the applicant explains the reasons for the switch. It is important to say what a year or two of college has given you, how you have grown. It is destructive to put down the faculty or academic quality of your current college. If the quality is poor then of what value are the A's earned there? You will need to study carefully the viewbooks of those colleges you wish to consider and rationalize and explain clearly why they are more appropriate for you than your present college. It is not enough to want to be at Ivy University just because you like ivy and prestige.

Transferring into highly selective colleges is difficult. For example, in 1989 Brown University accepted only about 100 students from among a transfer pool of about 750. For one thing, attrition is low at most selective colleges. Students who get in tend to stay. Secondly, some have freshman requirements, such as Columbia College's Contemporary Civilization course, which make transferring difficult when you have not had the same courses.

Sometimes the idea of transferring may seem right when, in fact, a more resourceful use of your current college's alternatives might make more sense in the long run. Most colleges have semester- or year-long options, foreign and domestic, that allow students to vary their experience without transferring. If you are tired of the woods or ski slopes, a semester in Washington, D.C., might give you the change you crave. Several colleges have exchange programs with other colleges where you will lose no credit, get a change of scene, and find the course you want in Egyptology. Often students at small colleges say that they need to broaden their social or academic possibilities. If you are enrolled at Haverford College, choices exist as exotic as Semester at Sea or as familiar as a course at nearby University of Pennsylvania.

If after thought and conversation with family and advisers you believe it is best to transfer, single out a few appropriate possibilities. As you did when you applied from high school, be sure to protect yourself with a list that includes a couple of fallback choices. Some transfer students believe that they would rather stay where they are if they cannot transfer "up." Others believe that they would rather be at their fallback in an urban area than stay in their rural environment with only 949 other students.

The decision to transfer is highly personal. You now have some college experience behind you on which to base your considerations. You should be more in charge of this decision than you may have felt as a senior in high school when peer and parental opinion carried more weight.

College indexes such as *Peterson's Guide to Four-Year Colleges* list transfer deadlines, some of which are as late as summer. In most cases, colleges will want to see at least one full year of results before making their decision, so you are unlikely to hear much before late May or early June.

Transferring in sophomore year rather than at the end of freshman year offers the advantage of putting up one full freshman year and a half or all of your sophomore year for spring or fall transfer, respectively. Not all colleges admit transfers in midyear.

You will need a letter from the dean of your college stating that you are in good standing and, usually, one or two letters of recommendation from faculty. Although interviews for transfer are rare, it's to your advantage if you can get one.

I recommend strongly that you look closely at all of the ways to diversify your current college experience as well as at alternative colleges that seem right for transfer. Before rashly applying to transfer, talk with teachers, advisers, or counselors whom you respect, so that they understand why you are thinking of doing so. Their opinion may help you to assess the wisdom of your proposed move. You will also want their support in the transfer process.

Once you are certain that a move is best, determine where you are more likely to succeed and go ahead with thoroughness, energy, and enthusiasm. Convince your prospective colleges that you know what you are doing and why.

Applicants from Foreign Countries

PPLICANTS to American colleges from foreign countries who have respectable academic credentials are of interest to admissions committees. They are even more interesting if they have scores over 600 on the Test of English as a Foreign Language and can pay their own way through college. When colleges began to fear declining enrollments in the late 1980s because there were fewer eighteen-year-olds in this country, they began to establish elaborate outreach programs to students from foreign countries. The motive was twofold: to continue to increase the diversity so important to the college experience, and to guard against empty dorms.

The steps I have outlined apply to foreign applicants as well; however, a foreign applicant competes only among a group of other foreign applicants. The drawback for the foreign applicant comes when a college is not familiar with the program or grading system of his or her particular school.

More responsibility falls on the foreign applicant to "translate" or interpret his or her academic program and record. Include a description of course content, either one issued by the school or one designed by yourself, including texts read in each course. In what language was instruction given? Does a class profile exist explaining how many received A's or C's in each class? What are graduation requirements, baccalaureate or advanced certificate examinations? Take the time to explain the content of your courses and what your grades from your school mean. Do not assume that this interpretation will be done for you.

It is important for foreign applicants to know the percentage of foreign students admitted by each college where they will be applying. Numbers, obtainable in a college index, vary considerably; for instance, at Columbia University foreign students comprise over 11% of the undergraduate student body, whereas at the University of Michigan, they make up under 7%. I advise that you make contact with the person responsible for foreign student admission; either write or phone to discuss your background and credentials and the advisability of submitting an application.

Transcripts and academic records must be in English. You will have to arrange for a translation through your school or through a private agency such as World Education Services, Old Chelsea Station, New York, New York, 10011.

If English is not your first language, you should register to take the Test of English as a Foreign Language, referred to as the TOEFL. The TOEFL is administered in the United States and in foreign countries by the Educational Testing Service. In order to register, you will need a Bulletin of Information; this will contain a registration form, calendar, and test centers. You can obtain a bulletin at a United States educational commission or foundation, binational centers, or a United States Information Service office. Certain countries require that you obtain the bulletin from the appropriate agency handling registrations from that country or area. You can get questions answered by contacting TOEFL, P.O. Box 6154, Princeton, New Jersey, 08541-6154.

The TOEFL exam is a multiple-choice test that takes three hours, and it is offered at over five hundred test centers in the United States and overseas six times annually. Plan to take the TOEFL at least five weeks earlier than the deadline for submitting your applications so as to avoid delays. The TOEFL is made up of listening comprehension, written expression, and reading comprehension sections. The registration bulletin contains sample questions. The written expression section measures your ability to recognize standard written English. The vocabulary and reading comprehension sections measure your ability to understand nontechnical reading passages. Several commercial publications such as *Barron's How to Prepare for the TOEFL* provide practice tests; some include recordings or cassette tapes so you can experience a listening comprehension section.

Many colleges in the United States offer summer and academic-year English-language training programs. These English as a Second Language (ESL) programs are authorized to issue Form I-20 to enable foreign students to receive a student visa (Form F-I Non-Immigrant Student Status). American embassies and consulates can provide lists of such accredited programs.

A few colleges with highly regarded ESL programs are

American Language Program
Columbia University
505 Lewisohn Hall
Columbia University
New York, New York 10027

American Language Institute
1 Washington Square
New York, New York 10003

These programs include intensive workshops in college-level English and writing and preparation for the TOEFL. There are two fourteen-week-long sessions in the spring and fall terms and an eight-week-long summer session.

American Culture and English Language Program for the
    College Bound
Manhattanville College
Purchase, New York 10577

Summer sessions combine academic, cultural, and recreational orientation to university life, including English-language instruction.

Language Institute for English
Fairleigh Dickinson University
Rutherford, New Jersey 07070-2299

The institute admits a new class every four weeks throughout the academic year. Students live on campus. This program is offered as well on the campuses of C. W. Post of Long Island University and of Dominican College of San Rafael in San Rafael, California.

Center for English Language Orientation Program
Boston University
Commonwealth Avenue
Boston, Massachusetts 02215

The program offers intensive English courses and orientation programs.

Some colleges offer their own English training program to students who are provisionally accepted.

Pitzer College, in Claremont, California, for instance, offers Programs in American College English for International Students (PACE), a twenty-two-hour-per-week curriculum of language skills. An international student may be admitted to Pitzer without a TOEFL if recommended by PACE staff and enrolled in PACE. The student is granted regular college status upon completion of PACE requirements and the recommendation of the PACE staff.

Florida State University, in Tallahassee, offers an intensive English program to students who do not score a minimum of 550 on the TOEFL and require additional English study.

Foreign student applicants will be asked, in their application, to have a bank verify that there are funds adequate to cover the cost of a four-year education in the United States. You will not be allowed to work your way through college in the States, nor should you expect a scholarship.

Once you have been accepted by an American college, and you decide to enroll, you will be sent an I-20 form. The I-20 and your passport will permit you to apply for a student visa from an American embassy or consulate. Be sure to check out your country's regulations on study abroad. Apply for your visa at the time you process college applications.

Foreign applicants need to give special attention to composing a written statement, including their reasons for wanting to study in the United States. Most American schools offer a less specialized program and a broader range of choice than foreign schools. You will need to say why you prefer the system in the States and particularly why you have chosen each college you apply to.

Be sure to allow for the mail delays between your country and the United States. If you plan and begin early, you will avoid much frustration. Use airmail, and when necessary express services, such as DHL.

Financial Aid

THE summer before my senior year in college in 1965, the fall tuition bill arrived at our house. The college announced an annual increase of $400, bringing the cost of tuition and room and board to $3,200. I remember my father saying, "Boy, am I ever glad you're almost through." Today my father would be even more relieved as tuitions alone at private colleges hover somewhere between $7,000 and $13,000. Housing adds another $2,500 to $4,000. Then there are personal expenses from laundry, books, and transportation to midnight pizza snacks.

For the past five years college costs have been rising at an annual average rate of between 7% and 8%. There is little reason to think that tuitions will level off. So long as enrollments remain strong, there is small likelihood of a downturn in cost.

In her excellent book on financing a college education, *How to Build a College Fund for Your Child,* Marion Buhagiar predicts that by 1999, based on a 7% rate of increase, it could well cost $25,780 for tuition at Amherst College or $26,134 for tuition at the University of Chicago per year. Public universities such as the University of Vermont could have tuition costs close to $7,000 as opposed to the current tuition of $3,400. At such a rate of escalation, total cost to attend Harvard University could run a family close to $60,000 annually!

College is now one of a family's major purchases and investments. More families than ever before will require some form of financial assistance.

Families are understandably confused and concerned about who will qualify for financial aid and about how much aid is really out there. Most want to know if applying for aid will hurt their son's or daughter's chance of being admitted.

Parents often want to protect their child from any mention or discussion of financial need. I believe strongly that the student needs to have an understanding of his or her family's financial situation. Discussions about financial aid are, in truth, a good chance to talk to your parents about how decisions are made within the family. While circumstances might not affect the choice of college in the long run, they may well call for certain sacrifices and efforts on the part of everyone in the family. A student has a right to know if he or she will need to work summers or on campus or accept a loan in order to make a certain college choice possible. Parents should be frank about what they will be able to contribute.

Applying to colleges is in itself a considerable expense. Most applications have a fee of between $20 and $50 to cover the cost of processing. The SAT is $15.50 per administration, the ACT $11.50, and the Achievement Test fee $22.00. Travel to visit colleges, test preparation courses, and fees for professional advice on the application process or financial aid, in addition to application costs, could well bring the cost of applying to $4,000 before any decision has been reached.

The value of a college degree in our society, however, continues to outweigh the concern aroused by such figures. We know by and large that college graduates earn up to 80% more in their first few years of work than those with only a high school diploma. As parents we want our children to have this advantage. We want them to qualify for jobs that pay well and offer possibilities for growth, advancement, and above all, personal satisfaction.

As college costs have risen, federally supported aid shrank by about 10% in the early 1980s. This still leaves the federal government the primary dispenser of aid. Most scholarship money comes from federal and state aid, the colleges, and plans paid by employers, not from private scholarship awards.

In recent years, the trend has been to expect families to provide the bulk of college costs. Therefore, you have to take an aggressive approach to discovering sources of financial aid. Start by planning early.

GETTING INFORMATION ABOUT FINANCIAL AID

Begin with a visit to your high school guidance or college counselor. Most high school counseling offices will have on hand basic college cost and financial aid information, such as *Meeting College Costs* published by the College Scholarship Service and available from the College Board at no cost.

Supplement your basic knowledge of financial aid by a visit to your local library's college reference section. Many books (see bibliography) are devoted to the topic of financial aid and contain indexes of specialized scholarships offered by industry and organizations for which you might qualify.

Consider making an appointment to visit a college financial aid office to speak with an aid officer who can help you.

You might also want to speak with a loan officer at a bank where you are known.

Never assume that you do not qualify for financial assistance. Seek the advice of professionals—accountants, financial aid officers at banks and colleges, and high school counselors. Joining these ranks is a new breed of professional who has sprung up in response to the overwhelming number of families who want information about aid. Financial planners now specialize in the subject of college costs and financial aid. They are knowledgeable about the various financial aid forms and will suggest specific strategies to help you.

Done well and with integrity, such advice can provide useful assistance with forms and with long-term financial management. No uniform standards exist to regulate such financial consulting firms, so families need to rely on the advice of guidance counselors or the Better Business Bureau to check out the reputation of a financial planner. Information from families you know may be the most reliable source for such recommendations. Avoid unethical manipulation or hiding of assets, as in most cases this will only set up unrealistic hopes about how much aid to expect.

Apply early for financial assistance, before funds are already appropriated.

Do not think that applying for financial aid will hurt an applicant's chances for acceptance by the college. If your child's qualifications match those of most applicants admitted to the college, you will not jeopardize your child's chances by declaring need.

Never rule out a college because of its cost. If your son or daughter is academically qualified, the application will be taken seriously. Some of the most expensive colleges are also the ones with the largest endowments, and they can afford to be generous with assistance, especially in the form of grants and scholarships. At the University of Chicago, Harvard, Stanford, and Macalester College, over half the entering freshmen receive some form of financial assistance.

Colleges have also devised creative payment plans of their own to offer their families. For instance, the University of Pennsylvania offers the Penn Plan, a tuition financing program with six different alternatives to suit a family's individual needs. Options range from a monthly payment plan at a modest annual interest that extends several years beyond graduation to guaranteed single-payment fixed tuition for all four years at the tuition set for the student's first year. At the University of Portland in Oregon, parents who do not qualify for financial assistance are permitted to defer a fixed amount of tuition over a two-year period at modest interest.

Financial aid comes in what is called a financial aid "package." A package includes grants or scholarships, which do not get paid back; loans, which can come from the federal government, a

savings and loan association, a credit union, a college, or a commercial bank; and work-study programs on campus.

PROCESSING THE FINANCIAL AID FORMS

Colleges determine the amount of financial aid needed based on
an analysis of a family's financial situation done by the College
Scholarship Service. *

A family completes the Financial Aid Form (FAF) sponsored by
the College Scholarship Service, or the Family Financial Statement (FFS) sponsored by the American College Testing Program.
Check to see if a college prefers one form over the other. Forms are
available from high school guidance offices.

The forms ask you to list income, assets, and liabilities. After
W-2 forms arrive and as early as possible in January, the form is
mailed to the College Scholarship Service or the American College
Testing Program. Time is very important in filing for financial
assistance.

Based on the form a need analysis emerges, which includes an
estimate of the maximum amount a family can be expected to pay
toward the cost of college.

The financial aid forms must be filed annually for aid to continue.

Under federal law, in split families only the income of the parent
with whom the child resides most of the time must submit financial information. The colleges, however, can and usually do require disclosure from each parent. The income and assets of a
stepparent must be disclosed with that of the natural parent.

Be sure to make photocopies of all financial aid forms. In this
process the burden is on you to do everything correctly.

* Almost all financial assistance is based on need. Quite naturally, need is the difference
between the cost of attending college and a family's ability to contribute toward that cost as
determined by need analysis. The amount a family is expected to contribute remains a
constant. The need at each individual college will, of course, vary according to overall cost.

The Parts of a Package

FEDERAL GRANTS

The main source of grant money is the Pell Grant. The grant may provide up to $2,300 per year if the family contribution is below $1,900 as assessed by the need analysis form.

Colleges expect anyone who files for financial aid at least to apply for the Pell, even if you do not expect to qualify. You cannot qualify to receive other awards unless you have been turned down first for a Pell. Check the Pell box on the financial aid form.

The second source of federal grants is the Secondary Educational Opportunity Grant (SEOG). These federal funds are administered by the college financial aid office and range from $200 to $4,000 per year for families with exceptionally high need.

OTHER GRANTS

Twenty-seven states offer grants as well; most are restricted to in-state college enrollment.

Other sources are private organizations, such as the Knights of Columbus and the Elks, as well as professional organizations, such as the American Meat Packing Industry or labor unions, which offer scholarships to children of members. For an extensive list of private grant sources, consult *Don't Miss Out* (see bibliography).

LOANS

Repayment schedules may require installments as early as sixty days from the time the loan is issued or as late as six months after completing a graduate program.

The Perkins Loan. Colleges determine who qualifies for these federal funds made available to the student. Students may qualify for up to $9,000 over the course of college. The annual rate of interest is 5%, and repayment begins six months after graduation and may be extended over ten years.

Stafford Loans. Stafford loans are determined by a local bank, credit union, or savings and loan association. There is no interest while the student is in college, and repayment begins six months after graduation or after completion of an accredited graduate program. Interest rates are 8% for years one to four and 10% after the fifth year. The loan may be extended up to ten years.

PLUS Loans. Parents Loans for Undergraduate Students is a federally funded program that gives parents the opportunity to borrow up to $4,000 per year per child at a variable interest rate with a 12% cap. Repayment begins sixty days after the loan is made.

COLLEGE WORK-STUDY PROGRAMS

The federal government subsidizes most jobs and the college the rest. A typical work requirement is ten hours per week at at least minimum wage.

Colleges also offer qualified students campus jobs, such as grading assistants or library attendants.

SUMMER EMPLOYMENT

Students who request aid are expected to use part of their summer earnings to pay for their education.

OTHER SOURCES OF AID

Military Scholarships

At over one thousand colleges and universities, the Army, Navy, Marines, and Air Force offer a Reserve Officers Training Corps program (ROTC). In addition to a regular academic course load, an ROTC student agrees to study military or naval science, or aerospace studies, depending upon the branch of service, and to take part in regularly scheduled military drills. An ROTC student also agrees to take part in up to three six-week summer sessions, and after graduation to go on active duty from six months to four years. In return, the ROTC program will pay for tuition, fees, and books, plus a stipend of $100 per month.

Privately Funded Scholarships

Many colleges offer scholarship money that you qualify for, if you have demonstrated need, just for being you.

At Washington University in St. Louis, the Taylor K. Castlen Scholarship Fund is limited to lineal descendants of persons who served in any branch of the U.S. armed services during WWI, WWII, or the Korean conflict.

At Washington and Lee in Lexington, Virginia, the Benjamin Hobson Frayser Scholarship gives preference to an orphan, of Confederate lineage, who is preparing for a career in medicine or the ministry.

At Colgate University, in Hamilton, New York, the Class of 1952 Arthur Mearns Scholarship gives preference to sons, daughters, and grandchildren of members of the Class of 1952.

At Wesleyan University, in Middletown, Connecticut, CIGNA awards money annually to two outstanding minority students, one from Hartford, Connecticut, and one from the Delaware Valley.

At Oberlin College, in Oberlin, Ohio, the Florence May Snell Scholarship is awarded to a woman beyond freshman year who shows scholarly promise and plans to teach, preferably in the field of English Literature.

At Hamilton College, in Clinton, New York, the Leavenworth Scholarship is to be awarded only to a student with that same surname.

At Lewis and Clark, in Portland, Oregon, varying amounts of

money are awarded to students with demonstrated achievement in debate and forensics.

Such scholarships are highly individualized—and sometimes eccentric. But it pays to scan college catalogues to see if your particular background or talent makes you a match. In most cases, your financial aid from other sources will be reduced if you are granted one of these special scholarships.

Some colleges offer family plans wherein a reduced tuition is offered to family members enrolled in the college concurrently. Some colleges also offer discounts to children of alumni and alumnae.

Private Agencies

There do exist private lending agencies that offer loan and install-ment payment plans, such as the following:

Academic Management Services:
50 Vision Boulevard
P. O. Box 4506
East Providence, Rhode Island 02914

This service will set up a budget plan and remit payments to college on a monthly basis for a fee of $45.

SHARE
NellieMae
50 Braintree Hill Park
Suite 300
Braintree, Massachusetts 02184

This agency provides loans of up to $80,000 for students who attend a group of affiliated colleges. For a list of member colleges, call 1-800-634-9308. Interest rates vary monthly but have a cap of prime rate plus 2%.

Advanced Placement Examinations

Students who accrue Advanced Placement credit in high school by taking AP exams each May in subjects in which they are qualified and score high (usually a 4 or a 5 on a scale of 1 to 5) can opt to complete college in three years. This could save up to a year's college cost.

AP scores can also be used toward credit, which can save partial cost.

Scholarships Based on the PSAT Results

The results of the PSAT taken in junior year are used to determine who will compete in the National Merit Scholarship Program and in the National Achievement Scholarship Program for Outstanding Negro Students. Out of the over one million students who take the PSAT, about fifteen thousand become semifinalists and over thirteen thousand will qualify as finalists. About six thousand of these are awarded Merit scholarships. Finalists compete by filing a form, writing a short essay about their interests, activities, and educational goals, and sending current grades.

The National Hispanic Scholar Awards Program sponsored by the College Board provides scholarships to over two thousand students who declare themselves of Hispanic background on the PSAT registration.

Achievement Scholarships

Some four-year colleges offer academic scholarships based on merit. For example, St. Lawrence University in Canton, New York, offers fifty need-based merit awards to those in the top 10% of their high school class with a 3.4 minimum average and SAT scores of 1200 or over or an ACT score of 28 or above. Kenyon College in Gambier, Ohio, offers twelve non-need-based awards for students in the upper 1% of their class and a grade point average of 3.5 or higher and SAT scores of 1350 or higher or an ACT score of 30 or above. Each year Tulane University in New Orleans, Louisiana, recognizes one hundred highly qualified freshmen with full tuition grants. These winners have demonstrated outstanding scholarship, talent, community involvement, and leadership. If your attendance at a college is dependent upon an academic scholarship make sure it is renewable each of four years.

Many highly competitive colleges, such as Amherst and Harvard, adhere to the decision made by the Eastern Group of Admissions Directors opposing no-need or merit-based scholarships.

As parents begin to apply for financial assistance, if they encounter any obstacles or need questions answered they should not hesitate to call the financial aid office at the college where their son or daughter is applying. Single parents with custody often have special concerns about how much responsibility the other natural parent will need to assume. In cases where a parent refuses to cooperate with demands for disclosure of financial information, the parent with custody may want to discuss circumstances by letter or in person with a financial aid officer at the college. There is no guarantee that exceptions can or will be made, but if a college really wants a student to enroll, it may be able to offer a compromise that will make that possible.

Families often ask if they must apply for financial assistance at the time the candidate applies for freshman admission. Some colleges insist that a family apply to receive aid in the freshman year if they hope to receive aid in later years. Some colleges acknowledge that circumstances change and are more willing to evaluate financial need year by year. It is important to become familiar with an individual college's financial aid policies. Do not assume you know how it administers aid; find out for sure.

For Students, but Especially for Parents

THIS section is for both college applicants and their parents. Parents have an important role as educators and sources of support in the college application process. So much of what will happen during the course of senior year will depend in part on the relationship between parents and their son or daughter. Some parents may have to learn to put confidence in their children's ability to make decisions, because young adults want respect for their choices. And choosing a college is a highly personal matter. The process requires self-evaluation, which can affect self-esteem. One minute an applicant may appear overly confident, sure he will be admitted everywhere, the next a shy retreative or a hostile reminder of the terrible twos. Moods shift quickly. On one day the student prepares to leave home and be more on his or her own and the next day he or she wants nothing more than to be hugged and given direction. It is a difficult time for parents to know when to be around and when not to be, when to speak and when to listen. When in doubt, be around and listen!

Parents are often confused by the changes in their son's or daughter's behavior during the college application process. The responsible student develops the habit of turning papers in late; the obedient child becomes a highly resistant young man or woman (suddenly getting Susie to wake up for school on time becomes a daily battle). During senior year students often experience a need for closeness and intimacy that throws them together with unlikely friends. As they fear being wrenched away from the familiar, they often engage in atypical behavior, such as drunk driving, promiscuity, and other "high-risk" behavior meant to shock or draw negative attention.

The only antidote to constant misunderstanding during this time is open and active dialogue—between parents and children, and among parents, children, and the professionals lending support. Parents should never underestimate what terror the application process holds for even the most seemingly sophisticated and outwardly cool senior. Let's look at some reasons why the process is so threatening.

To most teenagers the world seems full of possibilities. They believe that they can make anything happen, and the chance to compete is equated with the right to win. Our society has taught them that there is little to be learned from failure. For many, the college application process introduces the realization that life is not always fair.

Hardly an April fifteenth passes that decisions by colleges do not horrify us yet again with legendary tales about the student who had all A's in honors courses, high test scores, an editorship, and three varsity letters who was turned down by top colleges. A far larger population increasingly disappointed in the application process are the seniors who fall in what is called the "gray area" of college admissions. They have B averages, are solid citizens, have taken demanding courses, not necessarily at the Advanced Placement level, and have combined SAT scores of 1130 to 1180. They have done all the right things, but there is little to distinguish them in a very highly qualified pool at a selective college. Then there are those students who are bright underachievers. For one reason or another, they have not been able to realize their academic capabilities. They believe they can do the work at "a good college," yet fewer and fewer selective colleges are able to take risks on this type of long-term promising student.

Many seniors, even those with acceptances in hand, when asked how they feel about the process, respond with negative impressions:

"just a big game," "hell on earth," "frustrating and disillusioning."
They are cynical, as they see academically qualified tuba players
and lacrosse guards beat out valedictorians through campus gates.
Somewhere in between junior and senior years, expectation for so
many students turns to cynicism, disappointment, and anger at the
mixed messages and inequities in the process. They feel pushed
along by a system that compels most of them to continue from high
school to college without always exploring creative alternatives
such as an interim year or productive experimentation as an intern
or nontraditional student, be it an Outward Bound program or
study abroad. Students' needs and individual differences are frequently sacrificed so they can apply with credibility to "name
schools." What often happens in the process is that by trying to fit a
pattern they lose individual interests and characteristics that might
have made them stand apart from the crowd. They begin to feel
appropriately resentful that everything (including the student) is
perceived as a package.

The college application process may be the closest thing our
society has to a primitive rite of passage. It signals the move from
dependency and adolescence to self-reliance and young adulthood.
Seniors swing from the realization that adventure and change lie
before them to the acknowledgment that much of importance will
be left behind. Their moods range from excitement to fear, from
wanting independence to avoiding it. By its very nature, coming
when it does in their development, the college process is both a
blessed and a cursed event.

Seniors tend to view where they go to college as the most important decision of their lives. This belief is fueled by parents and
sometimes by those of us who guide seniors if we idealize and
glorify college life. We must be careful not to paint a prestigious
college as a ticket to a successful life. The experience of college also
brings with it, wherever one goes, its own uncertainty and home-
sickness. Students' sense of self is harshly tested as they experience
new demands, friends, and challenges. The word "college" uttered
at the wrong time to seniors is so emotionally charged that it can

send them flying to their room with a resounding slam of the door. Reluctant to admit even to themselves how anxious it makes them feel, seniors often act out their anxiety in rude or hostile behavior.

The process of getting into college is highly charged with personal and emotional considerations that often have little to do with the issue of getting into college or with which college you attend. The process becomes the focus on which a whole range of emotional and family concerns come to bear. Getting into college is, among other things, about leaving home and preparing to enter the world beyond. It is about saying good-bye to childhood and looking ahead but casting frequent glances over the shoulder. It is, in short, a time of conflicted feelings. Yet, it is an exciting time of self-discovery and new beginnings for the whole family. Even the family pet will go through a readjustment period when your son or daughter leaves home. When our son left for school, his cat of seven years took to life in the sink bowl for one week, in what seemed like utter despair. We all grow and change as part of a family when one of our members leaves. I encourage you to talk about the feelings you are experiencing with one another and with school or outside counselors. The first step to understanding feelings is acknowledging them.

If family dinner on a regular basis is not a tradition at your house, senior year is the time to introduce it. This is not the time for college talk; in fact, mention application deadlines at your own risk! Family dinners provide a time to share stories of the day and memories, to remind ourselves that we are and remain a family despite differences of opinion.

As our children prepare to leave us and as we prepare to let them go (or let go of them!), we will regress from time to time as we move toward change. Chances are it will not be a smooth year. As parents we may well find that our most important role is to listen. Often we cannot prevent inevitable disappointment or failure in the process, but we can let our children know that we love them and that we care how they are feeling. It is too easy to confuse our own needs and dreams with those of our child. As parents we need to be careful not to overidentify with the upswings and downswings experienced by our child during senior year. They do need, however, to know that we take seriously what they are going through. I remember vividly a late-night chat with our son right before he was leaving for college. Issues of self-confidence and the territory ahead were part of a painful talk for all of us. At the end, he said, "I know you can't change what I am feeling, but it helps that someone else at least knows how I feel." Just by being there, we can lessen the isolation our sons and daughters feel during a time of change. We need to emphasize, and mean it, that college is just *one* important point, not *the* most important point, in their lives. Just as important as where they get in is how the experience of the college application process has taken shape. The path toward adulthood is, and will remain, different for each person. Our role is to help them get through it with their self-esteem intact. We need to resist speaking in terms of admissions statistics and help our children to leave illusions behind only as they also learn about their own individualism. At the heart of the admissions process stand people, not numbers.

Parents need to keep an open mind about college possibilities for their son or daughter. They should entertain colleges they don't already know about and take the time to update their knowledge of colleges. Avoid being interested in only big-name schools for your own ego. Concentrating on prestigious colleges is unfair to the student who simply does not have the credentials to attend, or even the desire. Support your child's choices. If a family has planned carefully, there should be no college on the list that you would not accept as your child's school. Some choices may well be preferred, but each should have its merits. In April, when decisions are announced, help your son or daughter to feel pleased and accomplished by praising his or her acceptances, not conveying disappointment that the big ones got away. Parents who are very vocal about how disappointed they feel are inadvertently undermining any feelings of success their child might have. It is the candidate's credentials, after all, that have been evaluated. Take satisfaction in your son's or daughter's getting into a college where he or she is likely to do well, grow intellectually and socially, and prepare for a career. If conversation among yourselves breaks down at this point, as it often does, visit the counselor and get the viewpoint of an objective third party.

Let me conclude this book with a true story, one I often use to end my talks about college admissions, because it captures so well how quickly young people change their minds and how resilient they are. Tony had spent the spring of his junior year and most of senior year believing that if he did not attend Dartmouth College, his life would not be worth living. His family and all of us who worked with Tony did everything we could to help him make his dream come true. April of senior year arrived and so did a thick envelope from Dartmouth containing Tony's acceptance. In February of Tony's junior year at Dartmouth I received the following letter.

> Dear Dr. Leana,
> Just thought I'd mail off a quick letter from California to interrupt your day filled with frantic seniors.
> I made the wisest decision of my two-year college career a few months ago when I decided to take a transfer term out here at the University of California, San Diego. I love Dartmouth, but cold weather gets me down. It's like early summer out here, and I'm freaking out on the sun and the beaches.
> I have been taking a recreation class in massage, of all things. This has held my interest, primarily because it's co-ed. In a couple of years I could be the best educated masseur in the country.
> The fog's starting to lift, so I have to continue work on my tan. Californians take the sun for granted. They wouldn't last a minute in the Northeast.
>
> Take care,
> Tony

Suffice it to say, things change.

Calendar of Application Procedures

THE following calendar is to remind you of the steps you should be taking from October of junior year through the end of senior year to increase your chances for admission to college:

JUNIOR YEAR

October:

Take the Preliminary Scholastic Aptitude Test (PSAT). This examination is also used to determine National Merit Scholarship winners.

January–March:

1. Keep in mind that this will be the last *full* academic year before entering college. Grades count!
2. Discuss the wisdom of planning to take Advanced Placement examinations with the teachers of those courses. Sign up through your counselor.
3. Obtain a Social Security number.

April–May:

1. Look through *The College Handbook* and other similar guides to colleges (see bibliography). *The College Handbook*

is a handy sourcebook listing colleges' admissions procedures, median SAT scores required by individual colleges, application deadlines, as well as course offerings and tuition costs.

2. Make a spring visit to a college campus to evaluate its appropriateness for you. Look around, talk to students, and make inquiries. I generally do not recommend an interview at this early time.

3. Take the SAT and Achievement examinations. The SAT and Achievement Tests are offered on Saturday mornings concurrently; they cannot be taken on the same day. Sunday test dates are available for those whose Sabbath is Saturday. The ACT is administered on five dates each academic year.

Entering your name on the SAT registration form: Be sure that you always enter your name *exactly* the same way whenever you fill in an SAT, ACT, or Achievement form.

June–August:

1. Enjoy the summer expanding your interests and experience.

2. Visit colleges in which you have a strong interest, especially those that are far away. The more visits you make in the summer, the less time you will have to miss from classes during the first semester of the senior year. Senior year is extremely important academically, with demanding work, applications to complete, essays to compose. Too much time off only adds to the pressure. Over the summer, visit as much as possible and have interviews at those schools that interest you the most. It is more difficult to schedule appointments in the fall.

SENIOR YEAR

September–October:

1. Schedule a conference with a college counselor.
2. Send for any college applications you have not yet received or requested.
3. If you have decided to apply Early Decision to a first-choice college, plan to have your application submitted by November 1.
4. Decide which teachers (usually two) to ask to write recommendations for you. Hand them the forms that come with the applications. At the same time, provide properly addressed stamped envelopes. Teachers will mail their recommendations privately. Be sure to inform them of deadlines, especially if they are Early Decision or Early Action deadline dates. Be considerate; allow teachers sufficient time to do a good job, keeping in mind that each teacher has many such requests.

November:

1. Begin filling out college applications if you have not already done so; continue to work on them if you have.
   A. Be sure to meet the college's application deadline. The earliest deadline for regular admission is usually January 1.
   B. Be sure to pick up the appropriate cards for requesting the Educational Testing Service in Princeton, New Jersey, or the American College Testing Service in Iowa City, Iowa, to forward your test results to all the colleges. You can get these cards from your counselor.

C. Give your counselor a complete list of the colleges to which you will apply.

2. Register for any SAT, ACT, or Achievement Tests you have not yet completed. Engineering programs usually require one math and one science Achievement Test.

December–January:

1. If you are applying for financial aid, have your parents complete the FAF and submit it to the College Scholarship Service in Princeton, New Jersey, soon after January 1.
2. Complete your college applications.
3. Make remaining college visits and complete your interviews.

February–April:

1. As decisions are announced, discuss your final choices with a counselor and your parents.
2. Revisit colleges that have accepted you if you are having difficulty deciding which one to attend.
3. Notify colleges of your decision to accept or reject by May 1.

May:

1. Take those Advanced Placement examinations for which you are prepared. Examinations receiving a 3 or better (at some colleges, 4 or better) will count either for credit or toward sophomore standing.
2. Work to change Wait List status to an Admit.

June:

Enjoy graduation and have a great summer.

Selected Bibliography

The following books and indexes form the core of my counseling library. They are reliable, easy to use, and current. Indexes and most guides to colleges are updated annually; be sure to use the most recent edition. (Publication dates have been intentionally omitted from such indexes.) Most of these publications are available in bookstores, in school guidance or college counseling offices, and in the reference section of a public library.

Indexes

Barron's Profiles of American Colleges
   New York: Barron's Educational Series.

The College Handbook
   New York: College Entrance Examination Board.

Comparative Guide to American Colleges
   James Cass and Max Birnbaum.
   New York: Harper & Row, Publishers.

Peterson's Guide to Four-Year Colleges
   Princeton, New Jersey: Peterson's Guides.

Peterson's Guide to Two-Year Colleges
   Princeton, New Jersey: Peterson's Guides.

Specialized Indexes

Lovejoy's College Guide for the Learning Disabled
   New York: Monarch Press.

Peterson's Guide to Colleges with Programs for Learning-Disabled Students
    Princeton, New Jersey: Peterson's Guides.

Guides to Colleges
The Fiske Guide to Colleges
    Edward B. Fiske.
    New York: Times Books.

The Insider's Guide to the Colleges
    The Staff of *The Yale Daily News*, eds.
    New York: St. Martin's Press.

Courses by Major
Index of Majors
    New York: College Entrance Examination Board.

Financial Aid
The A's and B's of Academic Scholarships, 12th edition
    Janelle P. Adams, ed.
    Alexandria, Virginia: Octameron Press, 1989.

College Check Mate: Innovative Tuition Plans That Make You a Winner, 3rd edition
    Alexandria, Virginia: Octameron Press, 1989.

The College Cost Book
    New York: The College Board.

College Financial Aid Annual: How to Obtain Every Kind of Financial Aid for College
    John Schwartz, general ed.
    New York: Arco, 1989.

Dollars for Scholars
    Marguerite J. Dennis.
    New York: Barron's Educational Series, Inc., 1989.

Dollarwise Guide to American Colleges
    College Research Group of Concord, Massachusetts.
    New York: Arco, 1988.

Don't Miss Out: The Ambitious Student's Guide to Financial Aid, 14th edition
> Robert and Anna Leider.
> Alexandria, Virginia: Octameron Press, 1989.

Meeting College Costs
> Princeton, New Jersey: The College Scholarship Service of the College Board.

Paine Webber How to Build a College Fund for Your Child
> Marion Buhagiar.
> New York: Perigee Books, 1989.

Athletics
The Winning Edge: A Complete Guide to Intercollegiate Athletic Programs
> Frances and James Killpatrick.
> Alexandria, Virginia: Octameron Press, 1989.

General Reading about the Application Process
"College Bound"
> P.O. Box 6536, Evanston, Illinois 60204
> 312-262-5810

A newsletter of college issues and trends published six times a year.

Letting Go: A Parents' Guide to Today's College Experience
> Karen Levin Coburn and Madge Lawrence Treeger.
> Bethesda, Maryland: Adler & Adler, Publishers, Inc., 1988.

100 Successful College Application Essays
> Christopher J. and Gigi E. Georges, eds.
> New York: New American Library, 1988.

Scaling the Ivy Wall: Twelve Winning Steps to College Admissions
> Howard Greene and Robert Minton.
> Boston: Little, Brown and Company, 1987.

Summer Opportunities
Learning Vacations: The All-Season Guide to Educational Travel, 6th edition

Gerson G. Eisenberg.
Princeton, New Jersey: Peterson's Guides, 1989.

Summer on Campus: College Experiences for High School Students
Shirley Levin.
New York: College Board Publications, 1989.

Summer Opportunities for Kids and Teenagers
Christopher Billy, ed.
Princeton, New Jersey: Peterson's Guides, 1986.

A Taste of College: Summer Programs for High School Students on Campus, 2nd edition
Jane E. and David A. Nowitz.
Woodbridge, New Jersey: College Board Communications, Inc., 1989.

Study Abroad
Academic Year Abroad
E. Marguerite Howard, ed.
New York: Institute of International Education, 1989.

Describes over thirteen hundred study-abroad programs offered by accredited U.S. colleges and universities; also includes programs sponsored by foreign universities and language schools.